DATABASE CONCURRENCY CONTROL:
Methods, Performance, and Analysis

T0205459

The Kluwer International Series on
ADVANCES IN DATABASE SYSTEMS

Series Editor

Ahmed K. Elmagarmid

Purdue University
West Lafayette, IN 47907

The Kluwer International Series on Advances in Database Systems
addresses the following goals:

- To publish thorough and cohesive overviews of advanced topics in database systems.

- To publish works which are larger in scope than survey articles, and which will contain more detailed background information.

- To provide a single point coverage of advanced and timely topics.

- To provide a forum for a topic of study by many researchers that may not yet have reached a stage of maturity to warrant a comprehensive textbook.

DATABASE CONCURRENCY CONTROL:
Methods, Performance, and Analysis

by

Alexander Thomasian
IBM T.J. Watson Research Center

KLUWER ACADEMIC PUBLISHERS
Boston / Dordrecht / London

Distributors for North America:
Kluwer Academic Publishers
101 Philip Drive
Assinippi Park
Norwell, Massachusetts 02061 USA

Distributors for all other countries:
Kluwer Academic Publishers Group
Distribution Centre
Post Office Box 322
3300 AH Dordrecht, THE NETHERLANDS

Library of Congress Cataloging-in-Publication Data

A C.I.P. Catalogue record for this book is available
from the Library of Congress.

ISBN 978-1-4419-5161-8

Table of Contents

Preface

This monograph is a review of developments in concurrency control methods for centralized database systems, with a quick digression into distributed databases and multicomputers, the emphasis being on performance.

Database concurrency control has been an area of major research activity since 1975, which is reflected by the large number of contributions in this area. Most texts on concurrency control emphasize serializability theory (correctness) rather than performance issues [Casa81],[Papa86],[BeHG87],[CeGM88], [GrRe92],[LMWF94],[RaCh96]. There are a few texts, however, dealing with the performance of concurrency control methods. Tay's monograph is based on his dissertation [TayY87], while the concluding chapters in the text by Cellary, Gelenbe, and Morzy [CeGM88] outline analytical solutions to some rather abstract models of concurrency control methods. Recently a diverse collection of papers on this topic, some previously published, has appeared in a volume edited by Kumar [Kuma95].

The present monograph is based on the author's research in this area for the last fifteen years. The monograph is thus heavily influenced by his work and joint work with colleagues (see Acknowledgements). However, every attempt has been made to relate this work to others.

The main goals of the monograph are: (i) succinctly specify various concurrency control methods; (ii) describe models for evaluating the relative performance of concurrency control methods; (iii) point out problem areas in earlier performance analyses; (iv) introduce queueing network models to evaluate the baseline performance of transaction processing systems; (v) provide insights into the relative performance of concurrency control methods; (vi) illustrate the application of basic analytic methods to the performance analysis of various concurrency control methods; (vii) review transaction models which are intended to relieve the effect of lock contention; (viii) provide guidelines for improving the performance of transaction processing systems due to concurrency control; (ix) point out areas for further investigation.

This monograph should be of interest to researchers interested in concurrency control methods for high performance transaction processing systems, designers of such systems, and professionals concerned with improving (tuning) the performance of transaction processing systems. The monograph should be also valuable to researchers interested in performance evaluation of computer systems and especially database systems. Numerous areas requiring further investigation are listed throughout the text.

The reader is expected to be familiar with basic concepts in database management systems and concurrency control, as covered by the numerous textbooks on databases, including some of the aforementioned books specializing in concurrency control. Less preparation is required in the area of performance analysis. Sections 2.3 and 2.4 in Chapter 2 are intended to provide readers interested in performance evaluation with the requisite background in queueing theory, especially queueing network models, to understand the papers in this area. Although somewhat condensed, these sections should at least provide the reader with pointers to material in the numerous texts in this area [Klei75],[Koba81],[Triv82],[Lave83],[LZGS84]. Readers familiar with this area should skim these subsections, because of the backward references in Sections 3.4, 3.5, 4.4, and 5.5, which deal with performance analyses of the methods considered in the respective chapters. Sections 2.3.3-2.3.8 and 2.4 and the aforementioned sections can be skipped without loss in continuity.

An attempt has been made to make each chapter of the monograph self-contained and independent of other chapters, such that once the reader has read portions of Chapter 2, Chapters 3, 4, and 5 can be read independently of each other. There is a limited degree of redundancy in our presentation because of this reason. It is best to read Chapter 6 after reading Chapters 3, 4, and 5.

There are numerous references to figures and graphs in other works, which have not been reproduced here, in order to shorten the length of the monograph. Most readers are expected to have easy access to these references and over time accumulate a collection of relevant papers to supplement this monograph.

A short tag is used for references, which consists of the first four letters of the last name of the sole author, two letters from the last names of each of two authors, etc. followed by the year, and the letters a, b, ... when there are several papers by the author(s) for that year. This method of referencing gives a better clue to the identity of a paper than numeric references, while being less verbose and repetitive than mentioning the authors' names. The references are sorted according to the tag. This however affects the alphabetic ordering for the last names of a few authors in the reference list. References appearing in the text appear at the end of the regular index and serve as an alternative to an author index.

At the time of embarking on this effort it was realized that an all encompassing review is not possible due to (i) the vast literature on concurrency control methods; (ii) time constraints; (iii) the unavailability of translations of foreign language papers on the subject, although some papers have been republished in English. Only papers written in English are thus considered, but limited tracking of the (English) abstracts of non-English papers did not reveal any major new developments, especially beyond what had already appeared in the English versions of papers by the same authors.

Acknowledgements

This work has benefitted from the author's collaboration with In Kyung Ryu, previously a Ph.D. student at the University of Southern California, and Peter Franaszek and John Robinson at the IBM T. J. Watson Research Center.

The following individuals have encouraged my work in this area: P. Bernstein, J. Gray, H. Korth, P. O'Neil, Y. C. Tay, M. Rusenkiewicz, and G. Weikum. The idea for this work was suggested by R. Muntz while he was Editor-in-Chief of *ACM Computing Surveys*. Prof. A. Elmagarmid as Editor of Kluwer's Database Series expedited the text approval process. S. Delman, E. Kerrissey, and S. Rumsey from Kluwer Publishers were helpful in getting the text through.

Dedications

To the memory of my parents and my sister, and Mary E. Tobin's friendship.

"To search for perfection is all very well,
But to look for heaven is to live here in hell."

"Consider me gone" by Sting in "The dream of the blue turtles".

CHAPTER 1: INTRODUCTION

The requirement for *concurrency control* arose two decades ago to ensure correctness when a shared database is updated by multiple transactions concurrently [Ober80],[GrRe92]. Multiprogramming or concurrent processing of transactions in computer systems is required to take advantage of multiple processors and CPU-I/O (input/output) overlap to attain a higher transaction throughput.

The universally accepted correctness criterion for processing transactions against a database is *serializability,* i.e., the interleaved execution of a set of concurrent transactions should be tantamount to some serial execution [Date83],[Papa86],[BeHG87],[GrRe92]. This correctness criterion is not sufficient for some applications, e.g., stock trading bids may have a FCFS (first-come, first-served) processing requirement [PeRS88]. Such specialized systems will not be considered in this monograph. In fact correct executions need to be both serializable and recoverable when failures occur. A detailed discussion of these topics appears in [BeHG87],[GrRe92].

Standard locking, i.e., *strict two-phase locking* with on demand or dynamic lock requests and the *general waiting method* upon lock conflict, with some minor deviations, is almost exclusively used by current DBMSs (data base management systems) [Date83],[BeHG87],[GrRe92]. The *strict two-phase locking method* requires transactions to hold their locks up to their *commit* point, such that only committed data is exposed to other transactions, thus preventing cascading aborts [BeHG87],[GrRe92]. One of the aforementioned deviations is that shared locks are held for the duration of the corresponding read operation, which is referred to as *cursor stability* [Date83],[GrRe92]. Recovery from transaction failures is possible because the *write ahead logging protocol* writes the *before images* of modified data, which can be used for rollback [BeHG87],[GrRe92]. Data loss due to system failures with the No-Force commit policy is prevented by writing *after images* of committed data onto stable storage, e.g., disks [BeHG87],[GrRe92].

Two other widely discussed methods are *optimistic concurrency control* [KuRo81] and *timestamp ordering* methods [CePe84], [CeGM88]. Locking, optimistic concurrency control, and timestamp ordering methods are discussed in Chapters 3-4, 5, and 6, respectively. The *serialization graph testing* method maintains a *serialization graph* representing precedence relations among transactions, e.g., a transaction T_1 precedes a transaction T_2 if it has written a value which is read by T_1 [BeHG87]. Serializability is attained by ensuring that the graph remains acyclic, i.e., by aborting transactions to prevent cycles. This method allows all possible serializable executions, but is of little interest in practice, because cycle testing is computationally expensive.

We are mainly concerned with concurrency control methods for centralized, high-performance transaction processing systems, especially those with high levels of data contention. Concurrency control methods for multicomputer systems and distributed databases are also briefly discussed. A large number of concurrency control methods based on locking, optimistic concurrency control, and the combination of the two have been proposed in the last decade and it is the purpose of this monograph to succinctly describe these methods and provide insights into their relative performance.

A comprehensive hierarchical design methodology for database systems, including performance aspects is described in [Sevc81]. Our discussion of performance evaluation of transaction processing systems corresponds to the lowest layers of this hierarchy. A review of analytical modeling of the underlying computer system model for transaction processing systems is provided, since it is required for determining baseline system performance with no data contention. We also provide the performance analyses of several concurrency control methods to evaluate the effect of data contention on transaction performance and to illustrate the applicability of basic analytic techniques.

There is a degradation in performance due to concurrency control methods. The main source of which in the case of standard locking is transaction blocking upon lock conflict, while transaction aborts to resolve deadlocks tend to have a secondary effect on performance. A detailed analysis of standard locking is therefore provided, which takes into account transaction blocking due to lock conflicts, but ignores the effect of deadlocks. The simplifying assumption that lock requests are uniformly distributed over the lifetime of a transaction leads to a closed-form solution, which provides valuable insights into the *thrashing* behavior of standard locking, i.e., a severe degradation in performance due to transaction blocking.

Some concurrency methods use transaction aborts followed by (possibly delayed) restarts to resolve data conflicts. This results in increased response time and wasted processing, i.e., any processing not leading to transaction commit including transaction rollback overhead [GrRe92]. Thrashing due to excessive transaction restarts is possible with concurrency control methods, such as the basic timestamp ordering method [CePe84] and the no-waiting method [TayY87]. The degradation in performance in both cases is in the form of reduction in transaction throughput beyond a peak value as the degree of transaction concurrency is increased.

We discuss metrics to detect the susceptibility of a system with standard locking to thrashing, as well as how these metrics can be applied to load control. In the context of standard locking we introduce the *heterogeneous database access model,* which more realistically characterizes the workload of transaction processing systems (from the lock contention viewpoint) than the *homogeneous database access model,* which is used almost exclusively in performance modeling studies of concurrency control methods.

Two sets of methods are introduced to improve the performance of standard locking in high lock contention environments.

Restart-oriented locking methods utilize transaction aborts in addition to blocking upon lock conflict. Aborted transactions are restarted automatically. There is an improvement in overall performance in high lock contention environments provided there is spare capacity to accommodate the additional wasted processing. We consider the following restart-oriented locking methods: (i) the *no-waiting method* [TaSG85]; (ii) the *wound-wait* and the *wait-die* methods [RoSL78]; (iii) the *running priority method* [FrRo85],[FrRT92]; (iv) the *cautious waiting method* [HsZh92], (v) the *wait depth limited (WDL)* family of methods described in [FrRT92],[Thom92b],[Thom96] is a subset of other methods limiting the wait depth, which judiciously select the transaction to be aborted to minimize wasted processing. The wait depth is limited to zero in the case of the no-waiting method, and to one in the case of the symmetric running priority method [FrRT92], the symmetric cautious waiting method [Thom96], and the WDL method [FrRT92],[Thom92b],[Thom96].

Two-phase processing methods use an appropriate combination of the following execution modes: (i) *virtual execution* with no concurrency control, which only has a data prefetching effect [FrRT90],[FrRT92]; (ii) optimistic concurrency control [KuRo81]; (iii) locking. Additional execution phases are required when the first execution phase is not successful, e.g., failed validation with concurrency control. Two-phase processing methods with virtual execution or optimistic concurrency control in the first phase and locking in further phases can take advantage of *access invariance,* i.e., the property that a restarted transaction will access the same set of objects as it did in its prior execution [FrRT90],[FrRT92].

The monograph is organized as follows.

Chapter 2. We describe the transaction execution model, the database access model, and the computer system model in Section 2.1, 2.2, and 2.3, respectively. Variations from this model are introduced, when appropriate, in various chapters of this paper. Section 2.3 also describes analytic solution methods for evaluating the performance of transaction processing systems using queueing network models. In Section 2.4 we discuss methods generally used in the performance analysis of concurrency control methods, i.e., Markov chain methods and analyses based on mean values. We also comment on the level of modeling detail, separation of hardware and data resource contention, hybrid simulation methods, and issues in validating analytical solutions.

Chapter 3. We analyze the performance of standard locking, discuss its thrashing behavior, and describe several load control methods to prevent thrashing. We also provide two alternative analyses of lock preclaiming or static locking, i.e., acquiring the locks required by a transaction in advance. This is followed by a review of analytic solutions for dynamic locking. We introduce a more realistic locking model, followed by a discussion of some of the shortcomings of locking models. We then describe some recently proposed methods to reduce the level of lock contention. Finally, a brief description of locking as implemented in a commercial DBMS (IBM's DB2) is provided.

Chapter 4. We provide a succinct description of the aforementioned restart-oriented locking methods, including wait depth limited methods. We next discuss options for handling transactions restarts. The performance of restart-oriented locking methods is compared through simulation and we outline the analysis of the symmetric running priority method.

Chapter 5. We first describe optimistic concurrency control methods. Various transaction validation options and implementations are then discussed. A description of mechanisms used by two-phase processing methods is followed by some representative methods in this category. Simulation results to evaluate the performance of two-phase processing methods against each other and other methods are reported. Finally, we describe three related analytic solutions for optimistic concurrency control and outline the analysis of a hybrid method, which combines optimistic concurrency control and locking.

Chapter 6. This chapter briefly discusses concurrency control in distributed databases and data sharing systems [Rahm93b]. Techniques to improve performance in both cases are discussed.

Chapter 7. We point out areas requiring further investigation and mention some new areas where concurrency control is an issue.

The **Appendix** summarizes the notation defined in Chapter 2 and used in the analyses in further chapters.

CHAPTER 2: MODELING AND ANALYSIS OF TRANSACTION PROCESSING SYSTEMS

Methods for evaluating the performance of transaction processing systems as affected by hardware resource contention are described in this chapter. Hardware resource contention has the primary effect on performance, while data or lock contention has a secondary effect. In the case of blocking-oriented concurrency control methods, such as standard locking, the performance degradation is due to transaction blocking, while in the case of restart-oriented methods transaction response time deteriorates every time a transaction is aborted (we assume that aborted transactions are restarted automatically). The wasted processing due to transaction aborts adversely affects the response time of all transactions. Thus it is important to understand how hardware resource contention affects the performance of transaction processing systems, before considering the effect of data contention.

Relatively abstract models, both from the viewpoint of data and hardware resource contention, are used in most analytic and simulation performance evaluation studies of concurrency control methods. These models are not detailed enough for predicting the performance of "real" transaction processing systems, but are deemed to be adequate for the performance comparison of concurrency control methods. The choice of an appropriate level of modeling abstraction in analytic and simulation studies for this purpose remains an art. Abstract models tend to be less credible than detailed analytic or simulation models, while measurements from production systems and prototypes are at the other extreme of the credibility range.

Any amount of detail can be incorporated into a simulator, but modeling details may not yield new insights about the performance of a concurrency control method. Furthermore, a more detailed model increases coding time, complicates debugging, and increases the cost of running the simulation, especially to ensure that the performance measures obtained from simulation are statistically accurate (see Section 2.4.4 in Chapter 2). The level of detail required is dictated by the concurrency control methods being compared. Database buffers, for example, should be considered in evaluating the performance of restart-oriented concurrency control methods, which can take advantage of access invariance [FrRT90],[FrRT92] (see Chapter 5).

In Section 2.1 we describe the transaction model followed by the description of the database access models in Section 2.2. Section 2.3 is a description of a generic computer system represented by a queueing network model. This is followed by a brief discussion of the analysis of queueing network models. Finally, in Section 2.4 we describe solution methods based on Markov chain models and analyses based on mean values for evaluating the performance of concurrency control methods. We also comment on analytical modeling versus simulation, especially the validation of approximate analytic solutions. Readers not interested in analytic solutions of computer system models and analytical modeling may skip Sections 2.3.3-2.3.8 and 2.4. Also while the choice of topics covered in these two sections may seem eclectic, it is motivated by the techniques used in previous analyses of concurrency control methods.

2.1 Transaction Model

2.1.1 Transaction Structure

Single level transactions or *flat transactions* as opposed to *multilevel transactions* are of main interest in this study [GrRe92],[WeHa93] (other transaction structures are discussed in [Elma92],[RaCh96]). A transaction accessing k database objects consists of $k + 1$ execution steps, numbered $0 - k$. Each step involves CPU processing and possibly disk accesses. The last k steps begin with a database call, which leads to an access to a single database object, after an appropriate lock on the object has been acquired. This modeling assumption is made in most studies of concurrency control, although a database call may entail in accesses to multiple objects, requiring the acquisition of several locks (see Section 3.5 in Chapter 3). The completion of the last step leads to *transaction commit,* i.e., the writing of log records onto stable storage, after which the locks held by the transaction can be released [Date83], [BeHG87],[GrRe92].

Transactions can be classified as: (i) short update transactions, which read and update a few objects in the database; (ii) ad hoc queries requiring read-only access, usually at a reduced level of consistency [Date83],[GrRe92], [Moha92a]; (iii) batch updates, which read and update a significant fraction of objects in the database (see Section 4.11 in [GrRe92], [Baye86]). We are mainly interested in the first category and distinguish transaction classes based on their *size,* as determined the number of objects accessed by a transaction class, and their processing requirements. The fraction of transactions in class k (denoted by C_k) is f_k, $1 \leq k \leq K$ with $\sum_{k=1}^{K} f_k = 1$. The ith moment of the number of requested locks is $K_i = \sum_{k=1}^{K} k^i f_k$.

2.1.2 Transaction Arrival Process

Transactions originate from a finite number of sources (say S), which may correspond to bank tellers generating one transaction at a time and incur a "think-time" with a mean $Z = 1/\nu$ to generate the next transaction [Klei75], [Lave83],[LZGS84]. It is usually assumed that the think time has an exponential distribution $F(t) = 1 - e^{-\nu t}, t > 0$, which has the memoryless property, i.e.,

$F(t)$ does not change with the passage of time [Klei5],[Koba81],[Triv82], e.g., if lifetimes were exponentially distributed a 75 year old would expect to live for as many more years as a 5 year old. The arrival process with the *finite source model* is a *quasi-random arrival process* [Koba81] with an arrival rate $\Lambda(M) = (S - M)/Z$, when there are M transactions at the system and $S - M$ users in think mode. This transaction arrival model is adopted in some transaction processing benchmarks [Gray93]. For sufficiently large S the system can be considered to be an *open system* with Poisson or random arrivals. The number of arrivals (k) with a Poisson process in a time interval $(0,t)$ is given by $P_k(t) = e^{-\lambda t}(\lambda t)^k/k!$. Interarrival times in this case are exponentially distributed with rate λ and mean $1/\lambda$ [Klei75], [Koba81],[Triv82],[Lave83]. We furthermore assume *one-shot* transactions, such that the user is not involved after the transaction is submitted. Intervening user think times in a system with quasi-random arrivals, as in [AgCL87], result in an increase in the level of lock contention, which is due to the increase in the number of activated transactions holding locks.

The performance of an open system with random arrivals is characterized by the *response time characteristic* $R(\lambda)$ versus λ, while in the case of pseudo-random arrivals $R(S)$ versus S (for a fixed Z) or $R(Z)$ versus Z (for a fixed S) is of interest. When $Z = 0$ we have a *closed system*, where a completed transaction is *immediately* replaced by a new one. The performance measure of interest in this case is transaction throughput at a multiprogramming level or degree of transaction concurrency M, which is denoted by $T(M)$. The *effective throughput characteristic* is then $T(M)$, $M \geq 1$. The mean transaction residence time in the system is $R(M) = M/T(M)$ according to *Little's result* in queueing theory [Klei75],[Koba81], which states that the mean number of requests in a queueing system (the queue, server, combinations of one or more queues and servers) is equal to the product of the arrival rate of requests and the mean time they spend in the system [Klei75],[Koba81].

The seemingly unrealistic closed model is quite useful in comparing the performance of concurrency control methods for the following reasons: (i) the solution of a closed system can be used as a submodel in performance evaluation of an open system with external arrivals (see Section 2.2); (ii) it is easier to estimate the peak performance of some lock conflict resolution methods using a closed rather than an open simulation model, i.e., with fixed rather than variable number of transactions in the system, because the variability of the number of transactions in an open model may lead to thrashing at lower than expected mean system loads [Thom93b].

2.2 Database Access Model

The *database granule* is the unit of data at which concurrency control is applied to the database. Consider a database consisting of D granules, where each granule consists of g objects. A granule may correspond to a 4K database page, while the objects are 200 byte database records, i.e., $g = 20$. A fine locking granularity, e.g., at the record level, reduces the level of conflicts with respect to page level locking, but introduces complications when the unit of recovery is at the page level [GrRe92],[MHLP92].

Given the above model, we determine the mean number of locks required by a transaction accessing k objects from the $D \times g$ objects in the database. There are two cases depending on whether the objects accessed by transactions are replaced after the object is selected, such that the object can be selected again, or not. Given that the D objects in the database are accessed uniformly, in a *system with replacement* each granule is accessed with probability $1/D$. In a *system without replacement* the selection of all subsets of k objects from the $D \times g$ objects are equally likely. The mean number of granules touched in a system with and without replacement is given by the following expressions [LaSh82]

$$\bar{n}_{\text{with replac.}} = D\left[1 - \left(1 - \frac{1}{D}\right)^k\right],$$

$$\bar{n}_{\text{w/o replac.}} = D\left[1 - \binom{g(D-1)}{k} / \binom{gD}{k}\right].$$

The second term inside the brackets in both cases is the probability that a granule is not accessed. It is intuitively clear that (i) fewer granules are accessed in the former case, i.e., $\bar{n}_{\text{with replac.}} \leq \bar{n}_{\text{w/o replac.}}$; (ii) the two cases converge as $g \to \infty$ (for very large values of g the probability that the same object is selected is very small, which is tantamount to the with the replacement case); (iii) when D is large $\bar{n} \simeq k$ in both cases.

Performance analyses of concurrency control methods can be classified according to whether the objects accessed and especially locks obtained by a transaction are distinct or not, i.e., without and with replacement options [LaSh82], which is tantamount to whether the objects in an urn model are replaced after they are selected or not [Full68],[JoKo77]. The without replacement option seems more credible, but when transaction sizes are much smaller than the database size (D), results obtained by the above formulas are indistinguishable. This is because the probability that a transaction requests a lock on the same object is very small ($1/D$).

The analysis of the without replacement option leads to expressions based on binomial coefficients, which when simplified for numerical evaluation are tantamount to the expressions obtainable with the with replacement option. For example, the probability that k exclusive locks requested by a transaction are available when d locks are currently held in exclusive mode according to the without replacement option is given by

$$\text{Pr}[\text{requested } k \text{ locks available}|d \text{ locks held}] = \binom{D-d}{k} / \binom{D}{k}.$$

The computational cost of evaluating the binomial coefficients can be reduced by using the approximation $(1 - d/D)^k$, which corresponds to the expression we would have obtained directly with the with replacement option.

In a system without lock replacement, the probability $P_{lock}(k|n)$ that a transaction accessing n objects requires k locks can be computed using the following recursion with $P_{lock}(0|0) = 1$ [RyTh90a]:

$$P_{lock}(k|n) = \frac{kg - n + 1}{D - n + 1} P_{lock}(k|n-1) + \frac{D - (k-1)g}{D - n + 1} P_{lock}(k-1|n-1).$$

The distribution of the number of requested locks is obtained by unconditioning on the number of requested locks $P_{lock}(k) = \sum_{n=1}^{N} P_{lock}(k|n) f'_n$, where the fraction of transactions accessing n objects, f'_n, $1 \leq n \leq N$ is given. One method to simplify the analysis is to treat the mean number of locks as a fixed value, but this has the effect of underestimating the lock contention level and overestimating system performance (see e.g., [Thom93b]).

The effect of granularity of locking on performance has been considered in numerous studies (see e.g., Figure 3.10 in [BeHG87] and Figure 39(a) in [TayY87]). As the granularity of locking is varied from a very coarse to a very fine granularity there is: (i) an initial degradation in performance from serial processing (when there is only one granule) to a coarse granularity of locking, which is due to the high level of lock contention resulting in wasted processing to resolve deadlocks; (ii) an improvement in performance with a finer granularity of locking; (iii) a very fine granularity of locking may result in degraded performance due to increased locking overhead. *Lock escalation* can be used to reduce locking overhead, e.g., when the number of locks requested by a transaction on the pages of a table exceeds a certain threshold they are escalated to a table lock [Date83],[GrRe92],[IBMC95]. Most analytic studies do not consider locking overhead, which may be significant for long-lived transactions touching a large number of database objects. Locking granularity in the context of a commercial DBMS is discussed in Section 3.7 in Chapter 3. In what follows we do *not* consider the issue of granularity of locking, i.e., we assume that there is a lock associated with each object being accessed.

The *nonuniform database access model* or the *hot-spot database access model* can be expressed by the $b - c$ rule [TayY87], i.e., a fraction b (respectively $1 - b$) of transaction accesses are to a fraction c (respectively $1 - c$) of the database. Selecting $b + c = 1$ simplifies the comparison of the skewedness, e.g., the 80-20 law (with $b = 0.80$ and $c = 0.20$) is more skewed than the 75-25 law. A "self-similar" generalization of this rule appears in [Knut73], e.g., b^2 of accesses are to a fraction c^2 of the database, etc. The Zipfian distribution provides a good approximation to this distribution [Knut73].[1] The analysis of locking models with the skewed data access pattern is discussed in Section 3.4.1 in Chapter 3.

More generally, multiple database regions and transaction access patterns to these regions can be specified [Thom94a],[Thom95c] (see also Section 3.5.1 in Chapter 3). Nonuniformity of access has implications on other aspects of system performance [Chri84]. For example, a skewed access pattern to database objects will cause a higher level of lock contention, while resulting in a reduced number of disk accesses due to an increased buffer hit ratio.

An arbitrary data access distribution is considered in [SiYL94], such that p_i, $1 \le i \le D$ is the probability of access to the ith object in the database. Given that all lock requests are exclusive, the probabilities that M transactions have a lock conflict with each other and that a new transaction will have a conflict with M nonconflicting transactions is obtained in this paper using especially derived algorithms to reduce the computational cost. Numerical results show an increased probability of lock conflict as compared to uniform accesses.

The sequential granule placement or access pattern has been considered in some earlier simulation studies (see Chapter 4 in [TayY87]) and analytically in [RyTh88]. It corresponds to a strong degree of locality of access, e.g., rows of a relational database which are accessed through a "clustering index" [IBMC95]. Given k requests and g objects per granule, the number of granules touched is $\text{ceil}(k/g)$, which is the best case without replacement [LaSh82].

The random granule placement or access pattern is generally used in performance evaluation studies of locking methods. The assumption that all possible allocations of k accesses to D granules are equally likely is made in [PoLe80], but the probability that a transaction accessing k objects touches n granules from a total of D granules is derived using Bose-Einstein statistics, rather than Maxwell-Boltzmann statistics, which reflect a uniform distribution [Full68]. In fact Bose-Einstein and also Fermi-Dirac statistics are applicable to some elementary particles in physics, to which the more common Maxwell-Boltzmann statistics does not apply [Full68]. To illustrate the difference between the two statistics consider the assignment of 2 (indistinguishable) lock

---

[1] According to the Zipfian distribution $p_i = k/i^{1-\theta}$ and $k = 1/H_D^{(-\theta)}$, where $H_D^{(-\theta)}$ is the normalization constant (the Harmonic number of order $1 - \theta$). For the 80-20 law $\theta = \log_e 0.80 / \log_e 0.20 = 0.1386$.

requests (indicated by ″*″) to 2 granules. The three configurations |**||, ||**|, and |*|*| are equally likely according to the Bose-Einstein statistics, while the last configuration is twice as likely as others otherwise. The mean number of granules locked with $k = 2$ and $D = 2$ is $\bar{n}_{\text{with replac.}} = 1.5$, while for Bose-Einstein statistics $\bar{n} = kD/(k + D - 1) = 1.33$, i.e., in effect the level of lock contention is underestimated [LaSh82].

2.3 Computer System Model

An *infinite resource model* postulates that each transaction has its own virtual processor and can proceed at an execution speed independent of the number of active transactions in the system. Infinite resource models have been considered in some studies, especially those concerned with the performance limits of concurrency control methods [FrRo85],[TsPH86],[TayY87],[Thom93b]. A *finite resource model* allows the level of hardware resource contention to be varied to determine its effect on overall performance [AgCL87], [FrRT92],[Thom96]. Finite resource systems are represented by *queueing network models*, which can be used to determine transaction execution times as affected by hardware resource contention in a multiprogrammed computer system [Klei75],[Koba81],[Triv82],[Lave83],[LZGS84].

Section 2.3.1 is an introduction to queueing network models of computer systems, which is followed with a discussion of database buffering and logging for recovery in Section 2.3.2 [BeHG87],[GrRe92]. This is followed by the solution of *M/M/1* and *M/G/1* queues and open and closed queueing network models in Sections 2.3.3-2.3.5. The hierarchical decomposition method and the related hybrid simulation method (for queueing network models) are discussed in Sections 2.3.6 and 2.3.7. Finally, Section 2.3.8 is a commentary on the issue of separation of hardware and data resource contention in analyzing the performance of concurrency control methods.

2.3.1 Queueing Network Models for Computer Systems

The execution of transactions or *jobs* (in queueing network modeling terminology) in a computer system is represented by its transitions in the queueing network model which is a directed graph, whose nodes represent the devices of the computer system and the arcs represent the transfer of the locus of transaction execution from one node to another. This model implies that a job utilizes one device at a time. There are many situations when this assumption is violated [LZGS84], but it is reasonable for short transactions which tend to make random accesses to the database.[2] According to the *central-server model* of a computer system (as shown in Figure 1.1) the queueing network model consists of N devices, a CPU and $N - 1$ disks. A job starting at the CPU

---

[2] Anticipatory prefetching for long queries, which sequentially accesses data from relational tables introduces CPU-I/O overlap. The completion time of the query has been approximated in some studies by the maximum of the mean CPU processing time and disk access time, while a queueing network model would yield the sum of the two.

alternates between CPU execution and disk accesses, until it completes its execution at the CPU. Note that this is just a modeling convention associated with the central-server model, and a job can be considered completed after accessing the disk subsystem, e.g., for transaction commit purposes [GrRe92]. In a closed system a completed job is immediately replaced by a new job at the CPU, while in an open model the arrival time of the next job is determined by the interarrival time according to a random or quasi-random process, i.e., completion of a think time.

A probabilistic model is usually adopted, such that the probability of job completion at the CPU (versus additional disk accesses) is p_0, i.e., the number of visits to the CPU therefore has a geometric distribution $P_k = p_0(1 - p_0)^{k-1}$, $k \geq 1$ with a mean $v_0 = 1/p_0$ [Triv82]. The $N - 1$ disks are accessed with probabilities $q_i = p_i/(1 - p_0)$, $1 \leq i \leq N - 1$ with $\sum_{i=0}^{N-1} p_i = 1$. The mean number of visits to the ith disk is then $v_i = q_i(1/p_0 - 1) = p_i/p_0$, $1 \leq i \leq N - 1$. The transitions of jobs in the closed queueing network model can be specified by a *homogeneous Markov chain model* with N states, whose transitions are independent of the number of cycles already made [Klei75]. A *heterogeneous Markov chain model* for the state transition probabilities is utilized in some studies, e.g., in the case of the central-server model the transition probabilities are affected by the number of cycles a job has been through. In the case of a transaction processing system the number of cycles determines the number of accesses to database objects (possibly from disks), which are preceded by lock requests, i.e., a different transition implying transaction completion and the sending of a response to the user terminal is used after all locks have been acquired (see discussion of [IrLi79],[Thom82] in Section 3.4 in Chapter 3).

The *transition probability matrix* for the Markov chain is *stochastic* i.e., the probabilities in each row sum to one. In the case of the central-server model, the first row of the matrix corresponding to transitions from node zero -the CPU to itself (via the user terminals, which are ignored here) and to the $N - 1$ disks is $\underline{P}_1 = (p_0, p_1, ..., p_{N-1})$, while $P_{j,1} = 1$, $1 \leq j \leq N - 1$ for other rows specifies transitions from disks back to the CPU. The linear equations which would ordinarily yield the visit ratios $\underline{v} = \underline{v}P$ are not independent and an additional condition is required to determine them uniquely rather than within a multiplicative constant. In the case of the central-server model $\underline{v} = (v_0, v_0p_1, ..., v_0p_{N-1})$ satisfies the linear equations. Earlier, we used the argument that the number of visits of a job to the CPU is geometrically distributed to obtain v_0. Alternatively, the additional condition could have been obtained by including the terminals and noting that they are visited once.

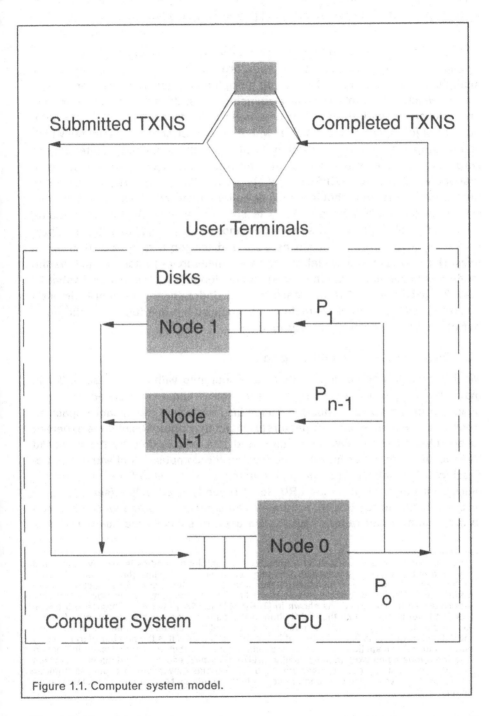

Figure 1.1. Computer system model.

The *mean service demand* or *mean loading* of a job at a node is its total service time at that node, which equals $X_n = v_n \bar{x}_n$, $1 \leq n \leq N$, where $\bar{x}_n$ is the mean service time at node n [Koba81],[Lave83],[LZGS84].

A queueing network model is *product-form*, which is amenable to a low-cost solution, provided that four node types are allowed: (i) a single server or multiple servers with a FCFS queueing discipline; (ii) *infinite servers* or a *delay server*, which do not introduce any queueing, as in the case of user terminals (in a closed network the number of servers should only equal the maximum number of jobs); (iii) a single-server with a processor-sharing discipline, which is a limiting case of the round-robin discipline with a quantum size tending to zero, i.e., n requests are served at $1/n$th of its capacity; (iv) the last-come, first-served discipline (LCFS) [Koba81],[Lave83],[LZGS84]. The service time for the first node type should be exponentially distributed, while it may have a general distribution for others. The solution of a product-form queueing network model requires the service demands X_n, $1 \leq n \leq N$ and the multiprogramming level (M) in a closed network and the job arrival rate in an open network to compute the usual performance measures of interest, such as the mean response time and the mean queue lengths at the nodes [Koba81], [Lave83],[LZGS84]. These measures are independent of more detailed queueing network model characteristics, such as the distribution of the number of cycles in the central-server model.[3]

2.3.2 Database Buffering and Logging

Most transaction processing systems are equipped with a *database buffer* in main memory, which obviates disk accesses when a referenced object is available in the buffer. Thus the *buffer hit ratio* has a significant impact on transaction response time. A page referenced in a prior execution is expected to be retained in the database buffer and to be accessible by the restarted transaction. The buffer hit ratio depends on the composition of workloads accessing the database and the *buffer management method*, i.e., a page replacement policy such as the LRU- least recently used policy (see [CoDe73] or Section 13.4 in [GrRe92]). A trace-driven simulation submodel can be used to determine the hit ratio, which is then used to estimate the number of disk

---

[3] The number of locks requested by transactions in simulation studies is usually associated with the number of disk accesses. A simulation study for validating the analysis of transactions with fixed size k is unsuitable if the number of cycles made by transactions is geometrically distributed with parameter $p_0 = 1/(k+1)$, i.e., the same mean transaction size as fixed size transactions. As shown in [ThRy91],[Thom93b] (also see Chapter 3) the lock conflict level is affected by the distribution of the number of requested locks, e.g., the geometric distribution introduces a much higher level of lock contention, than when the number of lock requests is fixed. Note that in the previous model it is the number of transaction steps and not transaction size which is geometrically distributed. As discussed in Section 3.4, the queueing network models used in [IrLi79],[Thom82] ensure a fixed number of cycles and lock requests by each transaction, by using job class switching to count the number of transaction cycles [Lave83] and in effect a heterogeneous Markov chain for state transitions.

accesses per transaction. Methods for analyzing the performance of memory hierarchies appear in [CoDe73].

The overhead associated with different concurrency control methods is expected to be comparable [Robi84]. In most studies this overhead is assumed to be included in the processing associated with transaction steps, but there is a dependence on the level of data contention, e.g., a lock request leading to a lock conflict and transaction blocking leads to additional CPU processing due to a context switch [RyTh90a]. The logging of commit data onto disk adds to the transaction response time and the holding time of locks.

A nonvolatile storage (NVS) for logging is postulated in some performance studies, such that the writing out of data onto disk (provided NVS space is not exhausted) can be deferred and carried out asynchronously. The impact of logging on transaction response time is then negligible. The NVS portion of the disk controller cache in a RAID5 disk array (see e.g., [Gibs91]) can be used for this purpose. Logging can be carried out efficiently by writing out large volumes of data to a dedicated logging device, almost fully utilizing disk bandwidth. Note that only log records need to be written out for a transaction to be committed according to the *No-Force commit method* [GrRe92], which does not require the dirty pages in the database buffer to be written onto disk for the transaction to commit. Dirty data blocks eventually migrate from the database buffer to the disk controller cache (sometimes as part of periodic checkpointing [GrRe92]). The writing out or *destaging* of these blocks from the disk controller cache onto disk can be carried out at a lower priority than disk reads, since read response time directly impacts transaction response time [Thom95a]. The numerical results based on the queueing analysis in [Thom95a] show that the impact of destages on read response times is minimal for some typical disk workloads up to very high overall disk utilizations.

2.3.3 Solution of M/M/1 and M/G/1 Queues

A single-server FCFS queue with Poisson arrivals (with rate λ) and exponential service times (with mean $\bar{x} = 1/\mu$) is referred to as an M/M/1 queue [Klei75],[Koba81], where the first (respectively second) M stands for Markovian or exponential interarrival (respectively service) times and one is the number of servers. The utilization factor of the server is the fraction of time it is busy, expressed as the ratio of mean service time and mean interarrival time: $\rho = \bar{x}/(1/\lambda) = \lambda\bar{x}$, or the mean number of requests at the server.

A birth-death model, is a continuous-time Markov chain with one dimension [Klei75],[Triv82],[LZGS84], whose states S_k represent the number of requests (k) at the M/M/1 queueing system. At S_0 the system is empty, at $S_k, k \geq 1$ the server is busy and there are $k - 1$ requests in the queue. The birth rates for all states are equal to λ, i.e., $S_{k-1} \xrightarrow{\lambda} S_k, k \geq 1$ and the death rates for all states (except S_0) are equal to μ, i.e., $S_{k-1} \overset{\mu}{\leftarrow} S_k, k \geq 1$. In this case we have a state-independent server, while for a state-dependent server we need to specify μ_k, $k \geq 1$. The steady-state probability that the system is at S_k is denoted by π_k. In equilibrium the flows in the two directions are equal,[4] which yields $\lambda \pi_{k-1} = \mu \pi_k$, $k \geq 1$ and $\pi_k = \pi_0 \rho^k$ in the case of state-independent servers. From the condition that the probabilities sum to one, we have $\pi_0 = 1 - \rho$, provided that $\rho < 1$. This condition is required for the steady-state solution to exist. If $\rho > 1$ then the system is saturated by an infinite backlog of requests. The system throughput in this case is $\mu(< \lambda)$, since the server is always busy. The number of requests in the system in steady-state has the geometric distribution $\pi_k = (1 - \rho)\rho^k, k \geq 0$ with a mean and variance $\overline{K} = \rho/(1 - \rho)$ and $\sigma_K^2 = \rho/(1 - \rho)^2$, respectively. Solutions for an $M/M/1$ system with state-dependent servers appears in [Klei75],[Triv82].

The mean response time follows from Little's result: $R = \overline{K}/\lambda = \overline{x}/(1 - \rho) = 1/(\mu - \lambda)$. The mean waiting time is $W = R - \overline{x} = \rho\overline{x}/(1 - \rho)$. More generally, in an $M/G/1$ queueing system with a general service time distribution $W = \rho\overline{x'}/(1 - \rho) = 0.5\lambda\overline{x^2}/(1 - \rho) = 0.5\rho\overline{x}(1 + c_x^2)/ (1 - \rho)$, where $\overline{x^2}$ is the second moment of service time, $\overline{x'} = 0.5\overline{x^2}/\overline{x}$ is the mean residual service time (mean residual lifetime in renewal theory terminology [Klei75]), i.e., the service time encountered by a random (Poisson) arrival from a sequence of service times when the server is busy (note that the probability that a service time is intercepted is proportional to its length and the associated probability), and $c_x^2 = \overline{x^2}/\overline{x}^2 - 1$ is the coefficient of variation squared [Klei75].

The mean waiting time encountered by an arrival is $W_{arr.} = \overline{K}_{queue}\overline{x} + \rho\overline{x'}$, where $\overline{K}_{queue}$ is the mean number of requests in the queue. Because Poisson Arrivals See Time Averages (referred to as PASTA) $W = W_{arr.}$ [Koba81],[Klei75]. Noting that $\overline{K}_{queue} = \lambda W$ yields W. In the case of the exponential service time distribution (an $M/M/1$ queueing system) $\overline{x} = 1/\mu$, $\overline{x^2} = 2\mu^{-2}$ and $\overline{x'} = 1/\mu$, which is consistent with its memoryless property. The distribution of the number of requests in $M/G/1$ queues and the waiting time distribution can be obtained in closed form for some distributions of service time. In the case of $M/G/1$ with processor-sharing discipline $R = \overline{x}/(1 - \rho)$, i.e., the mean response time is not affected by the variance of service time as in a FCFS server.

2.3.4 Solution of Open Queueing Network Models

The analysis of a product-form open queueing network model is simplified by *Jackson's theorem* [Klei75],[Koba81],[Lave83], which allows each node to be treated separately as if it is subjected to Poisson arrivals.[5] The throughput of

---

[4] This is a special case of the flow-in equals the flow-out from a state principle [Klei75].

[5] Arrivals to the nodes are Poisson when there is no feedback or cycles in job routing (as in the central-server model). This is because the output of individual queueing stations in this

the system equals the job arrival rate (λ), as long as $\rho_n = (\lambda v_n) \overline{x}_n = \lambda(v_n \overline{x}_n) = \lambda X_n < 1$, for $1 \leq n \leq N$, i.e., the utilization of none of the nodes exceeds one. The mean response time of a job is the sum of the mean residence times at the nodes $r(\lambda) = \sum_{n=1}^{N} r_n(\lambda)$. In the case of a single server with nodes with FCFS and processor-sharing disciplines $r_n(\lambda) = X_n/(1 - \rho_n)$, which is the mean response time in an $M/M/1$ system (with FCFS) or an $M/G/1$ system with the processor-sharing discipline [Klei75],[Lave83], [LZGS84]. In the case of a node with m servers (as in the case of a multiprocessor) $\rho_{CPU} = \lambda X_{CPU}/m$ and $R_{CPU} = X_{CPU}/(1 - \rho_{CPU}^m)$ for $m = 1,2$ (this expression has been used as an approximation for $m > 2$). The mean number of jobs in the system according to Little's result is then the product of the job arrival rate and the mean time spent by jobs in the computer system $\overline{M} = \lambda r(\lambda)$. Since the level of data contention tends to increase linearly with the number of transactions activated in a transaction processing system, the variability of the number of transactions in open systems makes them more susceptible to thrashing.

The device with the highest utilization in a queueing network model is referred to as the *bottleneck device* and its service demand determines the maximum throughput that can be sustained by the system $\lambda_{max} = 1/X_{bottleneck}$. The increase in $\overline{M}$ is quite rapid when the bottleneck resource in the system becomes saturated as λ increases, i.e., as $\rho_{bottleneck} \rightarrow 1$, $r_{bottleneck}(\lambda) \rightarrow \infty$ and hence $\overline{M} \rightarrow \infty$. Since the lock conflict probability increases proportionally to $\overline{M}$, there is a positive feedback effect, which may lead to thrashing. This is one of the reasons why open models are not suitable for studying data contention effects. This instability can be alleviated by enforcing a maximum multiprogramming level, i.e., in effect adopting a closed model. As a rule of thumb CPU utilization in a transaction processing system should be limited to 70% at peak load.[6] Note that this does not preclude the CPU from being fully utilized by additional lower priority work. A similar rule-of-thumb for random accesses to disks is that disk utilization should not exceed 30%, but obviously higher disk utilizations are acceptable with the presence of an NVS cache, which allows reads to be processed at a higher priority than writes (see Section 2.3.2).

Transactions which differ from the viewpoint of their processing requirements at the CPU or accesses to the disk subsystem should be mapped to different *job types* in the queueing network model of the computer system [Lave83],[LZGS84]. In the case of FCFS servers the service time for all job types should follow the *same* exponential distribution. The analysis of a queueing network with multiple job types requires the mean service demands

---

case is Poisson. This can be shown using Burke's theorem for $M/M/1$ queueing systems [Klei75].

[6] This typically corresponds to the knee of the mean response time curve versus the arrival rate in an $M/G/1$ queue.

for different job types and the number of jobs in each job type if the network is closed or their arrival rates if it is open [Lave83],[LZGS84].

2.3.5 Solution of Closed Queueing Network Models

A closed product-form queueing network model with a single job type with M jobs can be solved using the *convolution algorithm* or *mean value analysis* yielding the system throughput ($t(M)$) or mean residence time ($r(M)$) and more detailed metrics such as the mean queue lengths at the nodes of the network [Lave83],[LZGS84]. System throughput can be expressed explicitly when a closed queueing network model comprising of single-server queues is *balanced*, i.e., $X_n = X, 1 \leq n \leq N$. The mean queue length at each node is $\overline{Q}_n(M) = M/N$, $1 \leq n \leq N$ due to symmetry and according to the *arrival theorem* for closed queueing network models [Lave83],[LZGS84] the mean queue length encountered by a job arriving at a node is *the mean queue length with one job removed from the system* (note that PASTA does not hold in a closed system), such that the observed mean queue length at node n is $Q_n(M-1) = (M-1)/N$, $1 \leq n \leq N$. The mean residence time at node n with FCFS or processor-sharing discipline is $r_n(M) = [1 + \overline{Q}_n(M-1)]X = (M+N-1)X/N$. The mean residence time in the system and the system throughput are $r(M) = \sum_{n=1}^{N} r_n(M) = (M+N-1)X$ and $t(M) = M/[(M+N-1)X]$, respectively.

The system throughput $t(M)$ initially increases linearly with M, but $t(M) \rightarrow 1/X$ as $M \rightarrow \infty$. It is interesting to note that $t(m)$, $m \geq 1$ is concave if all the nodes of the queueing network model are *state-independent* [LZGS84], i.e., their service rate does not vary with the number of requests at the node. A node with multiple servers is an example of a *state-dependent* server, since it execution rate varies with th number of jobs at the server. The asymptotic behavior also prevails in an unbalanced QNM with a mean service demand X_n and m_n servers at node n ($1 \leq n \leq N$). The maximum throughput in this case is $t_{max} = t(M) \rightarrow 1/X'_{bottleneck}$ as $M \rightarrow \infty$, where $X'_{bottleneck} = \max(X_1/m_1, ..., X_N/m_N)$ [Lave83],[LZGS84].

In the performance analyses in the following sections we assume that the *system throughput characteristic* $t(M)$ $M \geq 1$, which only takes into account the hardware resource contention is given. The effective throughput characteristic $T(M)$, $M \geq 1$ takes into account the effect of data contention, as well, consequently $T(M) \leq t(M)$, $M \geq 1$. The maximum effective throughput is the performance measure utilized in some studies to compare the relative performance of concurrency control methods, e.g., in Section 4.3 which is based on [Thom96]. Of the two methods which attain the same maximum throughput, the one which attains it at a lower degree of transaction concurrency is preferable, since it yields a lower mean response time. Alternatively, the mean response time characteristic (the mean transaction response time versus the transaction arrival rate) can be used for comparison.

The convolution algorithm is described in [Koba81],[Lave83] and a tutorial derivation of the appropriate recursive equations in systems with single and multiple job types with state-independent and state-dependent servers is given in [ThNa81]. The mean value analysis method for analyzing closed queueing network models utilizes the aforementioned arrival theorem. In the case of a single job type system with state-independent servers it can be specified as follows [Lave83],[LZGS84]. Initialize $\overline{Q}_n(0) = 0$ and repeat the following three steps for $1 \leq m \leq M$ (i) compute mean residence time at node $1 \leq n \leq N$ as $r_n(m) = [1 + \overline{Q}_n(m - 1)]X_n$ (in the case of an infinite-server node $r_n(m) = X_n$); (ii) obtain the system throughput $t(m) = m/r(m)$, where $r(m) = \sum_{n=1}^{N} r_n(m)$ is the mean transaction residence time in the system; (iii) compute the mean queue length at node n $\overline{Q}_n(m) = t(m)r_n(m)$, $1 \leq n \leq N$, which is then used in step (i).

When M is large the cost of the recursive solution can be reduced by using a fixed point iteration, referred to as the Bard-Schweitzer approximation [Lave83],[LZGS84]. For $1 \leq n \leq N$ initialize $\overline{Q}_n(M) = M/N$; set $\overline{Q}_n(M - 1) \simeq (1 - 1/M)\overline{Q}_n(M)$ in step (i) for mean value analysis; and iterate until convergence is attained. The linearizer iterative solution method is an improvement on this method [ChNe82],[Lave83]. The proportional approximation method (PAM) is a family of fast noniterative methods, which is also suitable for this purpose [HsLa88].

A closed queueing network model with two job types is specified by the number of jobs of each type (M_1, M_2). The system throughput characteristic is then given by $t_i(M_1, M_2)$, $M_1 \geq 0$, $M_2 \geq 0$, $i = 1,2$. The total system throughput is the sum of individual throughputs. The effective throughput characteristic in this case is similarly $T_i(M_1, M_2)$, $M_1 \geq 0$, $M_2 \geq 0$, $i = 1,2$. The two transaction classes corresponding to the two job types may be affected differently by hardware resource and data contention, such that a comparison based on the total transaction throughput $(T_1(M_1, M_2) + T_2(M_1, M_2))$ is not meaningful. The mean overall transaction response time characteristic for given fractions of transactions in the arrival stream and maximum degrees of concurrency in the two classes can be obtained for performance comparison using the hierarchical solution method described in Section 2.4.

Rather than specifying the number of transactions in different classes in a closed system, a *frequency based model* might be preferable [Thom93b]. According to this model a completed transaction is immediately replaced by a new transaction in C_k with probability f_k, which is independent of the class of the completed transaction. Denoting the number of transaction classes by K, we have $\sum_{k=1}^{K} f_k = 1$. Due to *conservation of transaction frequencies,* the fraction of transactions in C_k completed by the system equals the fraction of transactions in that class which entered the system, therefore $t_k(M) = f_k t(M)$. The mean overall response time is $r(M) = \sum_{k=1}^{K} r_k(M) f_k$ or from Little's result $r(M) = M / t(M)$. The mean number of transactions in C_k is $\overline{M}_k = t_k(M) r_k(M)$, $1 \leq k \leq K$ (these values can be used in analyzing the queueing network model). The frequency based model is preferable to specifying the number of transactions in the different classes if we are interested in comparing the relative performance of various concurrency control methods based on their effective throughput characteristic, since it ensures that the same transaction mix is completed in all cases.

Some analytic solutions discussed in the following sections postulate a simplified model, where all transaction steps have equal processing times. If the system throughput for processing transaction steps is $t'(M)$ then $t(M) = t'(M)/(K_1 + 1)$. Also denoting the mean processing time per transaction step by $s(M) = M/t'(M)$, the mean response time for transactions in C_k is $r_k(M) = (k + 1)s(M)$.

Instead of the system throughput characteristic, we may assume that the mean transaction residence time $r(m) = m/t(m)$ or its expansion specified as $\eta(m) = r(m)/r(1)$ is known. This technique is used in Section 5.5 in Chapter 5 in analyzing the performance of optimistic concurrency control methods. In the case of a balanced queueing network model $\eta(M) = 1 + (M - 1)/N$.

A realistic computer system model for transaction processing cannot be adequately represented by a product-form (open or closed) queueing network model. For example, the computer system model in [FrRT92] violates the criteria for a product-form queueing network model by assuming nonexponential service times at the CPU and disks,[7] CPU priorities, and transaction blocking due to lock conflicts. There are numerous approximation techniques for extending product-form queueing network models to analyze realistic models of computer systems, which have been incorporated in queueing network model solvers (see e.g., [LZGS84]). The accuracy of these approximate analytic solutions varies unpredictably with input parameters. Hence extending such

---

[7] The distribution of service time has little effect on mean response time at lower utilizations, which is guaranteed as long as the number of servers (e.g., processors) equals M. This is because the mean residence time in a delay or infinite-server model equals the mean service time [Lave83],[LZGS84]. A smaller number of processors are also acceptable, especially in a closed system, as long as the number of requests at the CPU node rarely exceeds the number of servers.

solutions with approximate data contention analysis makes the determination of sources of approximation errors difficult. This was the main reason for adopting the simulation approach in [FrRT92].

The system performance degradation due to concurrency control methods is caused by transaction blocking, restarts, or both, as follows:

1. *Blocking-oriented concurrency control methods.* Such methods mainly use blocking to resolve data conflicts. Standard locking is the key concurrency control method meeting this criterion, since transaction aborts to resolve deadlocks are rare and the wasted processing introduced in this case is negligible. The probability mass function for the number of active transactions in the system is denoted by $\pi(m)$, $1 \leq m \leq M$. Transaction throughput and the mean number of active transactions in the system is

   given by $T(M) = \sum_{m=1}^{M} t(m)\pi(m)$ and $\overline{M}_a = \sum_{m=1}^{M} m\pi(m)$, respectively.

   Most analyses of standard locking only yield $\overline{M}_a$ (see e.g., [TaGS85],[Thom93b]). Provided that the system throughput characteristic is not highly discontinuous, we have $T(M){\simeq}t(\overline{M}_a)$. Since $t(M)$ is defined for integral values of M, we may use the rounded value of $\overline{M}_a$ or use interpolation: $T(M) = (\overline{M}'_a - \overline{M}_a)t(\overline{M}''_a) + (\overline{M}_a - \overline{M}''_a)t(\overline{M}'_a)$, where $\overline{M}'_a = \text{ceil}(\overline{M}_a)$ and $\overline{M}''_a = \text{floor}(\overline{M}_a)$.

2. *Restart-oriented concurrency control methods.* Such methods use aborts followed by system initiated restarts rather than blocking to resolve data conflicts. Optimistic concurrency control methods fall into this category (see Chapter 5). The efficiency factor $U(M)$ in a system with M transactions is the fraction of useful processing, i.e., processing leading to successful transaction validation and its commit. $U(M)$ in the case of optimistic concurrency control can be determined by the analysis in Section 5.5 in Chapter 5. It follows that $T(M) = U(M)t(M)$.

3. *Concurrency control methods which utilize blocking and restarts.* The running priority method [FoRo85],[FrRT92], which is analyzed in Section 4.5.4 in Chapter 4 belongs to this category. Combining the two sources of performance degradation and noting that the wasted processing is due to active transactions, we have $T(M){\simeq}U(\overline{M}_a)t(\overline{M}_a)$. The aforementioned analysis yields $U(\overline{M}_a)$ indirectly as $T(M)/t(\overline{M}_a)$.

   The method with the highest efficiency in this case may not be the method achieving the best performance. Guidelines for maximizing the peak system throughput in the context of restart-oriented locking methods is discussed in Section 4.3.

2.3.6 The Hierarchical Solution Method

The hierarchical solution method is useful in evaluating the performance of transaction processing systems with external arrivals, which cannot be solved directly as open models, e.g., due to constraints on the number of transactions that can be activated. The theoretical justification for this solution method is the *decomposition or aggregation principle in queueing network modeling* [Cour77],[Koba81],[Lave83],[LZGS84].

As an example of applying aggregation consider Figure 1.1. According to the equivalent of Norton's theorem in electrical circuits for queueing network models, the computer subsystem in the figure can be substituted by an *aggregate server* or a *flow-equivalent service center* [Lave83],[LZGS84]. In the case of a single job type (transaction class) the aggregate server is a *state-dependent* single server queue with a completion rate given by the system throughput characteristic $t(M)$, $M \geq 1$. The aggregate server has the processor-sharing discipline, since transactions in a multiprogrammed computer system are processed concurrently.

In case there are two transaction classes with different processing requirements, they should be mapped into two job types in a queueing network model. We can then compute the system throughputs $T_1(M_1, M_2)$, $T_2(M_1, M_2)$ for various combinations (M_1, M_2) of the two job types in the system. These throughputs then characterize the aggregate server.

Exact aggregation is possible when the overall queueing network model is product-form, such that a subnetwork can be substituted by an aggregate server. A major advantage of aggregation is that it tends to yield relatively robust approximations, when the overall queueing network model is not product-form, e.g., the maximum number of transactions that can be activated in the computer system is limited. Examples of applying aggregation in queueing networks appear in [ThNa81],[Lave83],[LZGS84].

Hierarchical analytic solutions typically consist of a lower level closed queueing network model, which is analyzed to obtain the throughput characteristic of the aggregate server which replaces the queueing network. This is accomplished by solving the corresponding closed queueing network model for all feasible job type combinations. The higher level Markov chain models job arrivals and departures, where job completion rates at its states are based on the throughputs of the aggregate server [Klei75],[Koba81],[ThNa81].

The higher level model for a system with a single job type is a birth-death model. The death rates from states S_M are given by the effective throughput characteristic $T(M)$, $M \geq 1$, which is the same as the system throughput characteristic ($t(M)$, $M \geq 1$) if there is no lock contention. In the case of random arrivals the number of states is infinite and the birth rate for all states is equal to λ. In the case of quasi-random arrivals there are $S + 1$ states with the birth rate from a state with M jobs given by $\Lambda(M) = (S - M)/Z$, $0 \leq M \leq S$. The birth-death model in these cases is analyzed by solving the state equilibrium equations.

When the multiprogramming level of the computer system is limited to M_{max}, a queue of jobs awaiting activation is formed for $m > M_{max}$.[8] This complication can be handled through an approximate analysis, which at first ignores this queueing effect and sets $T(M) = T(M_{max})$, $M \geq M_{max}$ in the birth-death model [Lave83],[LZGS84],[ThBa84]. The mean number of queued jobs and the mean number of activated jobs in the system is given by $\overline{M}_{queue} = \sum_{m > M_{max}} (m - M_{max})\,\pi(m)$ and $\overline{M}_{system} = \sum_{m > 0} m\,\pi(m)$, respectively, where $\pi(m)$ denotes the steady-state probabilities obtained by solving the birth-death model [Klei75],[Koba81]. The mean response time is $R = R_{queue} + R_{system}$ and for a system with Poisson arrivals (with rate λ) we have $R_{queue} = \overline{M}_{queue}/\lambda$ and $R_{system} = \overline{M}_{system}/\lambda$.

We distinguish transaction processing systems based on whether they are *hardware resource bound* or *lock contention bound*. In the former case peak transaction throughput (at M_{max}) is determined due to the saturation of the bottleneck resource, which may occur at a low lock contention level. Infinite resource systems with a sufficiently large M_{max} belong to the second category when the maximum throughput by a concurrency control method is attained at $\hat{M} < M_{max}$. The standard locking method due to its reliance on transaction blocking to resolve lock conflicts is least able to utilize hardware resources and is the most likely concurrency control method to lead a system to the second category [Thom93b] (also see Section 3.2 in Chapter 3). Lock contention bound systems are of a theoretical interest and are not expected to occur in practice. Transaction throughput $T(M)$ in a lock contention bound system increases with M reaching a maximum at $\hat{M}$, beyond which it drops. Using $\hat{M}$ as the multiprogramming level limit minimizes $\overline{M}_{system}$ (see e.g., Figure 3 in [WHMZ94]). In fact, simulation results show that the effective throughput characteristic remains flat up to $\hat{M}' > \hat{M}$, before dropping. The system response time obtained by using $\hat{M}'$ for the multiprogramming level limit is expected to be indistinguishable from that obtained using $\hat{M}$, since the reduction in $\overline{M}_{queue}$ is compensated by an increase in $\overline{M}_{system}$.[9] In addition, it follows from the discussion in Section 3.2 in Chapter 3 that the system is more susceptible to thrashing as M is increased beyond $\hat{M}$.

---

[8] This is an instance of taking into account *passive resources*, such as the main memory in the analysis. In fact database locks also belong to this category. *Multiple resource possession* in queueing network models has a slightly different connotation of requiring a secondary shared resource in order to utilize a primary resource, e.g., an I/O path (channel) is required in order to transmit data to/from disks [LZGS84].

[9] That this is so can be ascertained from the fact that the transition rates for both hierarchical models are the same, which implies the same mean number of transactions and mean response time. The hierarchical modeling method in this case, while approximate, tends to be quite accurate.

When transactions have different characteristics, a transaction processing system may enforce a maximum multiprogramming level on per transaction class basis or on combinations of transaction classes in *shared domains*. Efficient solution methods in the first case for open queueing network models with *population size constraints* are discussed in [ThBa84], while the latter case is discussed in [BrMc84]. The solution method in [Serr84] is applicable to more general constraints on transaction activation discussed in Section 3.5.

A system with multiple transaction classes with Poisson arrivals and pre-specified frequencies is considered. Static locking determines the combinations of transactions processible by the system, as given by a table [Thom85]. Mean transaction response times can be obtained by solving a multidimensional Markov chain, with the transition rates at each state given by the throughputs of the corresponding closed queueing network model with an appropriate composition of job types (transactions classes). One approach to reduce the computational cost is to utilize an additional level of aggregation based on the total number of transactions in the system [Thom85]. This yields a birth-death model, where the birth rate is the arrival rate of transactions and the death rates are $T(M)$, $1 \leq M \leq M_{max}$ and $T(M) = T(M_{max})$, $M > M_{max}$. The mean overall response time is then obtained by solving the birth-death model. The validation method used in this study is based on the numerical solution of the detailed Markov chain model (see e.g., [Stew78]). The difficulty of applying this technique is the effort required to generate the states of the Markov chain, hence the validation is carried out for small examples only. The hybrid simulation method, which is described below, is a more appropriate method to ascertain the accuracy of this approximation.

An example of the solution of a multilevel hierarchical model appears in [RyTh90a]. In this case a closed queueing network model with M transactions is solved to obtain the completion rate of transaction steps in a system with standard locking (the service demand at the CPU includes locking overheads). The per step throughputs are then used to obtain transaction throughputs $T(M)$, by taking into account the effect of lock conflicts and transaction aborts to resolve deadlocks. The effective throughput characteristic $T(M)$, $M \geq 1$ is then used in a birth-death model to obtain mean transaction response times in an open system.

2.3.7 The Hybrid Simulation Method

The hybrid simulation method models job arrivals and departures, while ignoring detailed job transitions in the queueing network model of the underlying computer system processing transactions. Use is made of job completion rates which are precomputed by solving the closed queueing network model for all feasible execution states [Schw78],[BDH+84]. The theoretical justification for this technique is again the hierarchical decomposition principle in queueing network modeling. In case there is a single job type, we obtain the system throughput characteristic by solving a closed model $t(M)$, $M \geq 1$. This discussion is applicable to multiple job types, where the time of the next transaction completion in a system with the combination of two job types (M_1, M_2) is $t_1(M_1, M_2) + t_2(M_1, M_2)$ and the probability that the completed job is in type i is given by $t_i(M_1, M_2)/ (t_1(M_1, M_2) + t_2(M_1, M_2))$, $i = 1,2$.

In the hybrid simulation method, which is based on the hierarchical decomposition principle. jobs are specified by the number of cycles required for their execution, where a cycle corresponds to CPU processing and disk accesses, as in the central-server model. The mean time to complete a cycle is the mean residence time (computed by solving the appropriate queueing network model) divided by the mean number of cycles. Job progress is determined by the number of remaining cycles.[10] An application of the hybrid simulation method in [Schw78] to multiple job types appears in [Thom87] in the context of dynamic load balancing in a multicomputer system.

Hybrid simulation typically results in a significant reduction in the number of events to be considered with respect to a direct simulation, i.e., a significant reduction in simulation cost. In the case of a transaction processing system with lock preclaiming, for example, there are two events per transaction, its arrival and departure (the scheduling of an initially blocked transaction occurs as part of the post-processing of another transaction's departure). There is no need to simulate the detailed events associated with the processing of a transaction in the queueing network model of the computer system. The hybrid simulation method is also useful for generating transaction residence times (respectively lock interrequest times) for static (respectively dynamic) locking in [ThRy83] (respectively [RyTh90a]). In fact the hybrid simulation method is a good substitute for a purely analytical method when an accurate analysis is not available for the higher level model.

2.3.8 Separation of Hardware and Data Resource Contention

The separation of hardware and data contention is a desirable property, which leads to simplifications in the analysis [TayY87]. This separation is possible in the context of the hierarchical solution method, if the transaction processing requirements on the hardware resources of the computer system are independent of the degree of transaction concurrency. This is so when the overhead associated with data contention is negligibly small and can be ignored. This separation means that the effective throughput characteristic need be

---

[10] The distribution of the number of cycles does not affect the mean response time of the aggregate server, since it behaves as an $M/G/1$ processor-sharing queue, i.e., the mean response time of transactions is determined by the mean number of cycles and is independent of its distribution. The exponential assumption for generating transaction completions according to the decomposition method is tantamount to a geometric distribution for the number of cycles.

computed only once, taking advantage of the fact that the convolution and mean value analysis methods yield the performance measures for all intermediate values, e.g., $T(m)$, $1 \leq m \leq M$ in the case of the throughput of a network with M jobs belonging to a single job type.

This technique is not applicable if the data contention overhead is significant. Extra processing is required in static locking to check for the eligibility of transactions blocked in a queue for activation [PoLe80],[ThRy83] (see Section 3.3 in Chapter 3). In the case of dynamic locking there is extra processing to block and later reactivate transactions encountering a lock conflict [RyTh90a]. Since the degree of lock contention is not known a priori, an iterative solution method is required which combines the analysis of the hardware resource model with the lock contention. One method to reduce the solution cost is to use fast methods for solving queueing network models, i.e., only for the multiprogramming level of interest to the analysis (see Section 2.3.5).

In the case of restart-oriented methods, such as the no-waiting method [TaSG85], there is the additional processing overhead due to transaction aborts, e.g., to rollback transaction updates, which is in addition to wasted processing. Separation of data and hardware resource contention is possible provided that the overhead for aborted transactions can be ignored. Otherwise, the noniterative solution of the no-waiting method in [TaSG85] should be combined with the solution of a queueing network model, in an iterative solution which takes into account restart overhead.

2.4 Analytic Solutions and Their Validation

Analysis is especially useful when it yields a closed form solution, which can be manipulated by standard mathematical methods to gain insight into the performance of concurrency control methods (in the case of standard locking see e.g., [TayY87],[Thom93b]). While abstract models are more amenable to analytic solutions, very few models lead to a closed-form solution.

Asymptotic expressions for the probability of blocking by arriving transactions, which preclaim their locks and with blocked transactions cleared, are derived in [Lave84],[Mitr85]. It is more realistic to assume that transactions encountering a lock conflict are enqueued, but this assumption complicates the analysis significantly (see Section 3.3 in Chapter 3). An outcome of the analysis in [Lave84],[Mitr85] is that a system where a fraction f_x (respectively $1 - f_x$) of lock requests to a database of size D is in exclusive (respectively shared) mode can be substituted by a system with exclusive locks only to a database with size $D_{eff.} = D/(2f_x - f_x^2)$. This result concurs with the analysis in [TaGS85],[TayY87] (see Section 3.4 in Chapter 3).

Two examples of analyses which obtain bounds to system performance are as follows. Static locking is implicitly considered in [FrRo85] and [TsPH86], where lock contention is represented by the pairwise probability of lock conflict (p) between any two transactions. It is shown in [FrRo85] that in a system with M transactions the *effective degree of concurrency* (in this case the mean number of active transactions) is $E = M(1 - p/2)^{M-1}$, so that $E \to 0$ as $M \to \infty$. In the case of a strict priority method, such as the wound-wait method (see Section 4.1 in Chapter 4), the effective degree of concurrency is $E \leq (1 - (1 - p)^M)/p$, which has an upper bound equal to $1/p$ as $M \to \infty$. In the case of optimistic concurrency control (see Sections 5.1 and 5.2 in Chapter 5) $E \to \infty$ as $M \to \infty$. Thus for this simplified model with infinite resources the optimistic concurrency control method outperforms others.

In a system with Poisson arrivals and constant transaction processing times (equal to one), i.e., an infinite server model, the maximum transaction arrival rate λ_{max} that can be sustained with a pairwise probability of lock conflict p is $1/e \leq \lim_{p \to 0} \lambda_{max} \times p \leq 0.75$ [TsPH86].

While this monograph emphasizes performance aspects of concurrency control methods, it is less concerned with analytic solutions for concurrency control methods, which may constitute advances in performance analysis methodology, but contribute little to understanding the performance of concurrency control methods.

2.4.1 Markov Chain Models

The state space explosion problem in modeling locking methods is well known (see e.g., the Introduction in [RyTh90a]). Consider a standard locking system with M transactions, where each transaction requests k exclusive locks uniformly from a database with D locks. Each transaction consists of $k + 1$ exponentially distributed steps. Locks are requested at the completion of the first k steps and the last step leads to transaction commit and the release of all locks. The state of the system can be specified by M vectors, with one vector per transaction. Each vector consists of the identities of requested locks. An extra element associated with each transaction is set to zero if the transaction holds the last lock it requested and otherwise the position of the transaction in a FCFS queue for the lock. There is a *state-space explosion problem*, since a transaction which has acquired all of its locks can have $\binom{D}{k}$ possible states!

There is a tradeoff between the detailedness of the state representation, which affects the cost of solving the state equilibrium equations, and the difficulty of deriving the transition rates among the states, which depends on the degree of state aggregation. For example, the state transitions for the previous model can be determined trivially. While a number of less detailed state representations are possible, the number of active transactions in the system

$(1 \leq J \leq M)$ is chosen as the state representation in [RyTh90a]. The state transition probabilities (for the underlying discrete-time Markov chain [Klei75]) require lengthy derivations for this compact state representation, which is usually the case.

There is the additional tradeoff between solution cost and its accuracy, which can be determined via simulation. Simulations yield a confidence interval for a performance measure of interest at a certain confidence level [Lave83],[Triv82]. It is quite expensive however to obtain tight confidence intervals at a high confidence level (say 99%) at a reasonable cost.

Very accurate results for validation purposes can be obtained using detailed Markov chains models, but such models lead to a state explosion which makes them impossible to solve, as in the case of standard locking. An investigation in which the detailedness of the model was varied to determine its effect on the accuracy of results is reported in [ThNa93] for a serialization delay problem, i.e., jobs requesting locks one at a time in exclusive mode. This study is limited to rather small examples, which is not because of the computational cost, but rather due to the difficulty of generating the states of the Markov chain without specialized tools, such as those used in conjunction with stochastic Petri net solvers [MaCB84]. It is observed from this limited study that even a very coarse state representation yields acceptably accurate results for global performance measures, such as system throughput, as compared to exact results due to a very detailed state representation.

2.4.2 Equilibrium Point Analysis

The equilibrium point analysis method is suited for solving large multidimensional Markov chain models, by assuming that *the system is always at an equilibrium point (state)*, at which the rate of entering the state equals the rate of exiting the state (see Chapter 2 in [Tasa86]). This is expressed as a nonlinear equation, which has one or more solutions for equilibrium states. The reason that equilibrium point analysis can give a good approximation to a stable system is because the steady-state probability distribution is symmetric about the equilibrium point, which is ascribed to the *central limit theorem* [Tasa86]. Rephrasing the argument in the context of lock contention, the state J of a system with M transactions with standard locking can be approximated as the sum of M independent random variables with values 0 or 1, depending on whether a transaction is blocked or active, provided that the interference among transactions is not so strong. Therefore the equilibrium state occupancy distribution can be approximated by a Gaussian (normal) distribution, which is symmetric [Koba81],[Triv82]. According to the equilibrium point analysis method the expected value of a random variable, such as throughput, is approximated by its value at the equilibrium point. This type of analysis has been used heavily in modeling communication systems, but to a limited degree in analyzing data contention (see Section 3.4 in Chapter 3 for an outline of the analysis in [RyTh90a]).

The system is *stable* if it has one solution and *bistable* otherwise. Referring to Figure 2.2 in [Tasa86] (also see Figure 19 in [TayY87] and Figure 8 in [Thom93]). There are three cases:[11]

- A stable system with a globally *stable equilibrium point*.
- A bistable system with two locally stable equilibrium points and an *unstable equilibrium point*.
- An overloaded system with a globally stable equilibrium point.

More detailed discussions of this topic appears in [Cour77].

2.4.3 Analyses Based on Mean Values

This is the most common solution method for concurrency control methods and is based on specifying relations among the mean values of involved variables. This method is illustrated in Section 3.2 by the detailed analysis of standard locking.

Most analytic solutions of concurrency control methods are based on reasonable simplifying assumptions, e.g., that there are a large number of small transactions in the system and the size of individual transactions is much smaller than the database size, such that the mean number of locks held in the system can be approximated by M times the mean number of locks held per transaction.

Analytical solutions of restart-oriented locking methods implicitly assume that locks requested by transactions are resampled upon restart [Thom96]. Lock resampling has a secondary effect in the following cases: (i) standard locking, since deadlocks are rare; (ii) optimistic concurrency control methods, where the conflicting transactions commit and leave the system.[12] As discussed in Section 4.2 in Chapter 4, lock resampling upon transaction restart has a significant effect on the performance of restart-oriented locking methods.

Most analytic solutions of concurrency control methods lead to a set of nonlinear equations, which are solved iteratively to yield numerical results. There is no guarantee that the fixed point, if approached, is the only one, rather than a local one. The proof of convergence and uniqueness of the iterative solution method is the exception rather than the rule in such analyses

---

[11] We will refer back to this discussion in Section 3.3 in Chapter 3, where we discuss the thrashing effect in standard locking.

[12] There is a small possibility that multiple transactions are aborted by the same transaction, such that they will conflict upon restart. Thus maintaining the identity of the locks is required even in this case, but has a second order effect (see discussion in Section 5.2).

(see e.g., [ChGM83],[GaBo83],[RMRR92]). Experimental results show however that the iterative solutions tend to converge up to a certain data contention level, e.g., the thrashing point for the system in the case of locking (see Section 4.2 in [Thom93b]).

2.4.4 Validation of Analytic Solutions

Simulation is required for validating the accuracy of analytic solutions, i.e., to measure errors introduced by: (i) simplifying modeling assumptions; (ii) approximations in the analysis. The validation of analytic solutions can then proceed in two steps. Firstly by running the simulation with the simplifying assumption, e.g., lock resampling upon transaction restart, to detect possible errors in the analysis and to assess its accuracy in analyzing the simplified model. This validation should be followed by another validation using a simulator with more realistic assumptions, e.g., without lock resampling, to assess the error introduced by this assumption.

Once an analytical solution has been validated, it can be used for parametric studies. A thorough validation of an approximate analytic solution method to ascertain its robustness for a wide range of parameters is a non-trivial task. A solution method which is validated at lower data contention levels may be inaccurate at higher lock contention levels. The level of data contention is proportional to the multiprogramming level (M). Thus a closed system with limited hardware resources is unsuitable for validation, since the peak throughput is reached at smaller values of M, i.e., usually at a low data contention level. So what is the maximum value of M required to ascertain that the analysis is accurate? This can be accomplished by considering a closed system with infinite resources and validating the analysis up to the point at which the peak throughput is attained [Thom92b], [Thom93b], [Thom96]. Note that a solution method which is accurate for low to moderate lock contention levels is expected to be adequate for all pragmatic purposes, e.g., if such a solution is to be incorporated into a queueing network modeling package to evaluate the effect of data contention on the performance of transaction processing systems.

Finally, the analytic solution of a concurrency control method may predict a high level performance measure accurately for some set of parameters, while there are unacceptable errors in estimating lower level performance measures. In the case of a method which utilizes both transaction blocking and aborts, such as the running priority method [FrRo85], this may be due to a coincidental compensating effect, i.e., transaction blocking time is overestimated, while the fraction of aborted transactions is underestimated. A careful validation requires experimentation with a larger set of input parameters, as well as the validation of lower level performance measures.

A layered analysis with a clear delineation of levels systematizes the analysis, facilitates its presentation, and makes the validation process easier, see e.g., [RyTh90a]. This is because validation may be carried out in a bottom-up manner, to ensure that errors at lower levels do not propagate to higher levels (refer to Figures 4 and 6 in [RyTh90a]). Assuming that it is known from simulation results that the effect of deadlocks on the performance of the standard locking system is negligibly small [ThRy91],[Thom93b], then the analysis should take into account only the mean transaction blocking time, which equals the product of the mean number of lock requests per transaction, the probability of lock conflict (P_c), and the mean waiting time per lock conflict (W). Validation of standard locking requires the checking of the accuracy of estimates for these two performance measures, rather than just the mean response time. In case P_c is found to be inaccurate, the accuracy of estimates for lower level parameters, such as the mean number of exclusive and shared locks held per transaction, needs to be investigated. A bottom-up validation is not always possible, as in the case of analyses requiring an iterative solution method, since some variables can only be expressed as a function of other variables, e.g., in the case of $x = f(u, v, w, a, b)$ where a and b are input parameters, but u, v, w are also determined by the analysis. In fact approximate analytic solutions and validation can be carried out in an interleaved manner, such that the accuracy of an approximate expression for x is checked out immediately.[13]

The development of analytic solutions for concurrency control methods and their careful validation is a time consuming task, which has been usually carried out as part of doctoral theses or in research laboratories. In addition analytic solutions have numerous shortcomings, such as being based on unrealistic modeling assumptions and losing their accuracy at higher data contention levels. Given declining computing costs and the increasing abundance of computing resources, e.g., networks of workstations with appropriate software to utilize idle workstations, it has become possible to carry out extensive parametric studies using simulation (at an acceptable turnaround time and cost). An analytic orientation is valuable, however, in specifying the simulation model and assuring the validity of simulation results.[14]

---

[13] Some effort is required to instrument the simulator to measure and display a subset of variables. It would be best if the simulator is integrated with a data analysis tool to check certain relations among measured variables, e.g., an equation derived by the analysis. This would be helpful also in deriving new relations, e.g., by using regression analysis. An example of the application of this approach is the expression for the probability of deadlock derived in [LiNo82] based on simulation results. This expression, however, is different in form from expressions given in Section 3.1 in Chapter 3.

[14] Some early simulation studies of concurrency control methods suffered from the fact that they were carried out in the thrashing region for locking [LiNo82] or with over-committed hardware resources, e.g., a saturated CPU (see discussion in Chapter 4 in [TayY87]).

A case in point is the simulation study of optimistic concurrency control in a distributed database, where ignoring the effect of data contention, e.g., with all accesses in shared mode, fixed size transactions are outperformed by variable size transactions with the same mean transaction size [Thom92a]. A possible explanation for this is the observation from simulation results that fixed size transactions tend to access slightly more remote sites than variable size transactions. That this is truly so is ascertained by an analysis involving the application of Jensen's inequality [Klei75] for the particular model for remote site accesses (Bernoulli trials are used in [Thom93a] to determine whether a local or remote node is being accessed). This precluded the need for additional lengthy simulations.

Our discussion so far has been concerned with validating analytic studies against simulation results, while it would be more interesting to validate analytic or simulation results against production systems or at least transaction processing benchmarks (see [Gray90]), since they provide a more controlled environment.

Discrete-event simulation is apparently an easy method to compare the relative performance of concurrency control methods. Various methods to obtain confidence intervals, to ensure the accuracy of estimated parameters are described in [Triv82] and Chapter 6 in [Lave83]. The *batch means method* of repeating the experiment with different seeds (for random number generators) is most commonly used for this purpose. Familiarity with more advanced topics, such as *variance reduction* [Lave83] is beneficial in writing more efficient simulations.

As an application of variance reduction consider a simulation study to compare two concurrency control methods: (i) standard locking which is mainly based on blocking; and (ii) the no-waiting method, which aborts a transaction encountering a lock conflict. The fact that the no-waiting method results in relatively frequent aborts, while aborts to resolve deadlocks are quite rare with the standard locking method, will result in a different workload from the viewpoint of the lock request pattern if lock requests are generated on demand starting with the same initial seed for this purpose. To ensure that the same workload is processed in both cases we can generate the identities of *all* locks at the time a transaction is introduced into the system. Similar arguments apply to the processing time associated with transaction steps, especially when they are assumed to be independent of the system load.

CHAPTER 3: STANDARD LOCKING AND ITS PERFORMANCE

Locking is the concurrency control method used by almost all DBMSs. It is for this reason that the paradigm for "correct" transaction execution, i.e., two-phase locking was first stated in this context [EGLT76] (also see [Date83],[BeHG87],[GrRe92]). Two-phase locking simply requires that no locks be released before all locks are acquired,[15] but this scheme is susceptible to cascading aborts, since a transaction whose updates have been accessed by other transactions may itself be aborted. *Strict two-phase locking* prevents cascading aborts by deferring the releasing of locks acquired by a transaction to its *commit point*, [Date83],[BeHG87],[GrRe92]. Only the analysis of strict two-phase locking is considered in this chapter, as is the case with almost all studies of standard locking performance (see Section 3.6 for exceptions). The lock holding time is then from the instant at which the lock is requested to transaction completion time.

It is reasonable to assume that locks are requested on demand, which is referred to as *dynamic locking,* while in *static locking* all database objects re-quired for the execution of a transaction are assumed to be known a priori (before its execution is started) and that the transaction should acquire all locks before its execution begins. Static locking is possible at a course granularity, e.g., batch transactions predeclaring accesses to a subset of ta-bles in a relational database [Date83],[IBMC95]. Techniques based on trans-action pre-execution to determine the locks required by a transaction at a finer granularity of locking are described in Section 5.4 in Chapter 5.

Different options are available in dynamic locking when a transaction re-quests a lock held by another transaction, i.e., *a lock conflict occurs.* In this chapter we only consider the *general waiting* method, according to which a transaction making a conflicting lock request is blocked awaiting the release of the lock *if a deadlock has not occurred.* Methods utilizing a combination of transaction blocking and aborts in resolving lock conflicts are discussed in Chapter 4.

This chapter is organized as follows. We first consider standard locking with dynamic lock requests as in [Thom93b]. In Section 3.1 we derive the probability of lock conflict, probability of deadlock, and the mean blocking time per lock conflict with respect to an active transaction. In Section 3.2 we ana-lyze the two cases when transactions have identical and different processing times for their steps. These analyses demonstrate the thrashing behavior of dynamic locking, which is based on [Thom93b]. In Section 3.3 (respectively

---

[15] There is the additional requirement that locking modes cannot be downgraded, e.g., from exclusive to shared [GrRe92].

Section 3.4) we discuss analytic solutions for static (respectively dynamic) locking. This ordering is motivated by the chronology of papers dealing with the two cases, which is attributable to the fact that static locking is easier to analyze than dynamic locking, especially when the effect of deadlocks in dynamic locking is to be taken into account. In Section 3.5 we introduce a *heterogeneous* database access model and also propose a finite-state model for characterizing transactions. We also discuss some shortcomings of current locking models from the viewpoint of evaluating the performance of transaction processing systems. In Section 3.6 some variations to standard locking are described. A brief description of locking in DB2 is given in Section 3.7.

3.1 Lock Conflicts and Deadlocks

We consider the analysis of a closed system with standard locking as in [Thom93b]. The analysis of variable size transactions is an extension of the analysis of fixed size transactions considered first. We also include a brief discussion on deadlock resolution schemes.

3.1.1 System Operation

The execution of a transaction with dynamic locking with k lock requests (of size k) consists of $k + 1$ steps, at the beginning of the last k steps it makes a lock request, while at the end of the last step it releases all locks and commits (see Section 2.1.1 in Chapter 2). When a lock conflict occurs and there is no deadlock then the transaction is blocked according to the general waiting method and the lock request is enqueued in a FCFS queue. Although some systems carry out deadlock detection on a periodic basis [GrRe92], in the simulation study to validate the analysis deadlocks are detected and resolved immediately. This is facilitated by maintaining a *waits-for graph* [BeHG87], which is specified in Section 3.1.2. The selection of the transaction to be aborted has a secondary effect on performance, as has been verified in previous simulation studies (see Section 3.1.4), hence the transaction causing the deadlock is aborted by the simulator used for validation.

Several locking modes have been defined, especially in the context of relational DBMSs [Date83],[BeHG87],[GrRe92], but we only consider the analysis of a system with exclusive and shared locks. All lock requests are initially assumed to be in exclusive mode, while shared locks are considered in Section 3.4.1. Strict two-phase locking is used in all cases, i.e., exclusive and shared locks are held to the end.

A transaction holding a shared lock on a database object should promote it to an exclusive lock, before it can update the object. A deadlock will arise if this action is taken concurrently by several transactions holding a shared lock on the same object. According to [Gray80] (summarized in [Date83]) 97% of deadlocks in IBM's System R (a research prototype) are due to lock promotion (a similar discussion appears in [Kort83]). When the updating of an object is a possibility, deadlocks can be avoided by using update locks, which are only compatible with shared locks [Kort83],[Date83],[GrRe92]. Update locks can be converted to exclusive locks, but the conversion of shared locks to update and exclusive) locks is forbidden [Kort83]. The analysis of DB2 traces for several workloads reveals that approximately 90% of exclusive locks are obtained directly [SiSm94].

A more commonly known form of deadlock occurs when a transaction T_1, which holds an exclusive lock on object A (O_A) requests an exclusive lock on O_B, which is locked by T_2 in exclusive mode. T_1 is blocked as a result of the lock conflict. A deadlock occurs if T_2 next requests an exclusive lock on O_A. Several other scenarios also lead to a deadlock, e.g., if O_A and O_B were originally locked in shared mode. As shown later in this chapter, deadlocks involving multiple transactions are less frequent than two-way deadlocks.

3.1.2 Analysis of Dynamic Locking with Fixed Transaction Sizes with Identical per Step Processing Times

In the case of a system with lock contention the mean processing time per transaction step is given by $s(\overline{M_a})$, where $\overline{M_a}$ denotes the mean number of active transactions in the system. The mean number of blocked transactions is $\overline{M_b} = M - \overline{M_a}$. The mean blocking time per step is $u = P_c W$, where P_c is the probability of lock conflict (per lock request) and W is the mean waiting time (per lock conflict). Blocking time is assumed to be distributed equally among the last k steps of a transaction in C_k (class k), i.e., the mean duration of the first step (respectively last k steps) is $s(\overline{M_a})$ (respectively $s(\overline{M_a}) + u$). It follows that the mean transaction response time or more appropriately residence time (since we are dealing with a closed system) is $R(M) = (k + 1)s(\overline{M_a}) + kP_c W$ and the effective throughput is $T(M) = M/R(M)$.

Our analysis ignores the possibility of transaction restarts to resolve deadlocks, which are known to be rare [ThRy91],[GrRe92]. On the other hand equation (3.3) -given below- implies that the probability of deadlock increases with the fourth power of transaction size, which is a weakness of this analysis when very long transactions are allowed in the system. The effect of deadlocks is taken into account in [RyTh90a] (see discussion in Section 3.4), which assumes that the transaction causing the deadlock is aborted. On the other hand a sophisticated deadlock resolution method will attempt not to abort a transaction which has made significant progress in terms of acquired locks and hardware resource consumption (see discussion at the end of this section), but this will overly complicate the analysis (see e.g., [Thom92b]).

The mean number of locks held by a transaction of size k not encountering any lock conflicts is $\bar{L} = k/2$, which is the ratio of the time-space of locks held by a transaction and its mean residence time: $0.5k(k + 1)s(M)/[(k + 1)s(M)]$. In the case of a system with lock contention $\bar{L} \simeq k/2$, which is a very good approximation as verified by the simulation results in [RyTh90a] (see Table I).

We consider a system with M transactions and each transaction accesses k objects with uniform probabilities from the D objects in the database. It is highly likely that the accessed objects are distinct (selection without replacement), since we have postulated that D is much larger than k. When all lock requests are *exclusive* the probability of lock conflict (P_c) for the $i + 1$st lock request of a transaction is[16]

$$P_c = \frac{\text{Mean number of locks held by other transactions}}{\text{Number of locks in the database not held by the transaction}} =$$

$$\frac{\bar{N} - i}{D - i} \simeq \frac{(M - 1)\bar{L}}{D} \simeq \frac{(M - 1)k}{2D} \qquad (3.1)$$

where $\bar{N}$ is the mean number of exclusive locks held in the system. We have substituted the numerator with the mean number of locks held by the *other* $M - 1$ transactions in the closed system and in the denominator ignored the number of locks already held by the transaction. The latter approximation is based on the fact that transaction size $k(\geq i)$ tends to be much smaller than D [TayY87], [RyTh90a]. The probability that a transaction encounters a lock conflict is

$$P_w = 1 - (1 - P_c)^k \simeq kP_c \simeq \frac{(M - 1)k^2}{2D}. \qquad (3.2)$$

The approximation is justified by the fact that P_c tends to be very small (e.g., $P_c < 0.001$). The probability that two transactions are blocking each other and are involved in a two way deadlock is given in Section 7.11.5 of [GrRe92] as:

$$P_D(2) = \Pr[T_1 \to T_2]\Pr[T_2 \to T_1](\text{number of candidates for } T_2) =$$

$$\frac{P_w^2}{M - 1} \simeq \frac{(M - 1)k^4}{4D^2}. \qquad (3.3)$$

Similar expressions apply to multi-way deadlocks, but since P_w is very small, $P_D(i)$ for $i > 2$ is negligibly small. It follows that the probability of deadlock at the transaction level is $P_D = \sum_{i \geq 2} P_D(i) \simeq P_D(2)$.

The above analysis does not take into account the fact that the "other" transaction should be blocked at the time of the lock conflict for a deadlock to

---

[16] We ignore the dependency of P_c on the transaction step, as justified by what follows.

develop. The fraction of time transactions are blocked in the system (denoted by β) is the ratio of transaction blocking time and its mean response time, which is equal to the fraction of blocked transactions in the system

$$\beta = \frac{kP_cW}{R(M)} = \frac{\overline{M_b}}{M},\tag{3.4}$$

where the second fraction (the fraction of transactions blocked in the system) follows from Little's result by multiplying the numerator and denominator of the first fraction by $T(M)$ (the effective throughput with M transactions).

The distribution of the number of active transactions can be approximated by a modified binomial distribution $\pi(m) = \binom{M}{m} (1 - \beta)^m \beta^{M-m} / (1 - \beta^M)$, $1 \le m \le M$, since at least one transaction is always active if deadlocks are resolved immediately. Since $\beta^M \rightarrow 0$ for higher values of M, it follows from the resulting binomial distribution (with $0 \le m \le M$) that the mean number of active and blocked transactions is $\overline{M_a} = M(1 - \beta)$ and $\overline{M_b} = M\beta$, respectively.

Transaction blocking can be specified by a waits-for graph, which is a directed graph with nodes representing transactions and edges the waits-for relationships. In a system which only allows exclusive lock requests, the system state is representable by a forest of trees, where the nodes with out-degree zero represent active transactions. Designating the active transactions as level zero nodes implies that transactions blocked by active transactions are at level one. The directed acyclic graph need be appropriately extended to take into account shared locks, in which case we will have a forest of Banyan trees (a tree with multiple roots). Alternatively, the nodes of transactions requesting shared locks can be coalesced into one node, which is split into several nodes when the transactions becomes active again by acquiring shared locks.

A rigorous estimation of W is not an easy task, since the waits-for graph evolves over time. In a system with a low level of lock contention most lock conflicts are with active transactions, which is the only case of interest here, since we are interested in two-way deadlocks. The mean waiting time with respect to transactions blocked at level one (W_1) can be obtained by noting that the probability of lock conflict with a transaction increases in proportion with the number of locks that it holds, i.e., the probability of conflict at S_j is $j/(k(k + 1)/2)$, where the denominator is a normalization constant to ensure that the probabilities sum to one. This expression does not reflect lock holding times since they are assumed to be equal, but this is not the case for transactions with different step durations (see equation (3.14)). It follows that [ThRy91]

$$W_1 = \sum_{j=1}^{k} \frac{2j}{k(k+1)} \left[(k-j)(s(\overline{M}_a) + u) + s'(\overline{M}_a) \right] =$$

$$\frac{k-1}{3} \left[s(\overline{M}_a) + u \right] + s'(\overline{M}_a). \tag{3.5}$$

The term in the brackets is the processing time in the remaining steps after a conflict occurs at S_j and $s'(\overline{M}_a)$ is the mean residual processing time (see Section 2.3.3 in Chapter 2) of S_j. $s'(\overline{M}_a)$ equals $s(\overline{M}_a)/2$ when the processing time is fixed, $2s(\overline{M}_a)/3$ when it is according to a uniform distribution (as in [TayY87]), and $s(\overline{M}_a)$ when it is exponentially distributed.[17] A similar expression is derived in [TaGS85],[TayY87] and in [JeKT88] in the context of analyzing the effect of locking on the performance of a distributed database system.

The fraction of time that a transaction is blocked by an active transaction is $A = W_1/R(M)$. It follows from equation (3.5) that in the case of fixed size transactions $A \simeq 1/3$. The analysis in Section III.A in [ThRy91], which takes into account that T_1 should be in the blocked state for a deadlock to occur, yields $P'_D(2) = P_D(2)/3$ ($P_D(2)$ was given by equation (3.3)). Simulation results in Table I [ThRy91] show that this analysis is quite accurate in the case of variable and fixed size transactions. Note that the analysis in [GrRe2] yields $3P'_D(2)$, that in [Mass86] yielding $2P'_D(2)$,[18] and that in [TaGS85],[TayY87] yields $4/3P'_D(2)$.

The analysis in [ThRy91] proceeds to derive the expression for probability of lock conflict and deadlock when transactions are variable in size. The mean number of locks held by a transaction according to equation (3.8) (given below) is affected by the second moment of transaction size (lock request) distribution. The probability of deadlock per transaction is affected by the third moment of transaction size (see equation (17) in [ThRy91]) and for example, it is shown in [ThRy91] that this probability is an order of magnitude higher for the geometrically distributed transaction sizes with the same mean as fixed size transactions.

A periodic deadlock resolution method is used in some commercial databases such as IBM's DB2 (see Section 3.7). The mean number of blocked transactions in such a system will exceed that of a system with immediate deadlock detection and resolution. There is a secondary effect that transactions remaining blocked due to deadlocks cause further lock conflicts.

---

[17] The residual lifetime argument holds if the conflict rate with succeeding steps is the same, but this is not quite so since the probability of conflict increases with j. However, most conflicts occur with transactions holding a large number of locks, such that there is less sensitivity with respect to small increments in j.

[18] This analysis considers a table where the row number corresponds to distinct transactions in the system and the columns to the synchronously requested locks by these transactions. The analysis does not take into account previous transaction blockings due to lock conflicts.

Given the lock request rate and the probability of lock conflict and deadlock per lock request, it is of interest to estimate the number of deadlock cycles in the system at the end of the deadlock detection period. From the viewpoint of improving system performance, the duration of this period should be varied dynamically, such that the fraction of periods in which deadlocks are detected is small.

The detailed analysis to obtain the probability of deadlock in a system with two transactions, where a transaction may request multiple locks at the beginning of each step, is considered in [Reut95]. One of the conclusions of this study is that for a fixed transaction size (product of number of transactions steps and the number of locks requested in each step) the probability of deadlock increases for a larger number of transaction steps and fewer lock requests per step.

3.1.3 Analysis of Dynamic Locking with Variable Size Transactions

While variability in transaction sizes is expected, most performance studies of standard locking consider fixed rather than variable size transactions, since this assumption simplifies the analysis. The mean response time for transactions in C_k, which constitute a fraction f_k of the transactions processed by the system is $R_k(M) = (k + 1)s(\overline{M}_a) + kP_cW$ (this expression is obviously applicable to a system with a single transaction class of size k), from which the mean overall response time follows:

$$R(M) = \sum_{k=1}^{K} R_k(M)f_k = r(\overline{M}_a) + K_1P_cW, \tag{3.6}$$

where $r(\overline{M}_a) = (K_1 + 1)s(\overline{M}_a)$. Since $\beta = K_1P_cW/R(M)$ it follows that[19]

$$R(M) = \frac{r(\overline{M}_a)}{1 - \beta}. \tag{3.7}$$

Alternatively, as shown in Section 2.3 of Chapter 2, the effective throughput can be obtained from the system throughput characteristic $T(M) \simeq t(\overline{M}_a)$, because the wasted processing due to deadlocks is negligibly small. That $T(M) = t(\overline{M}_a)$ and $R(M) = R(\overline{M}_a)/(1 - \beta)$ do not contradict can be shown by setting $T(M) = M/R(M)$ and $t(\overline{M}_a) = M(1 - \beta)/r(\overline{M}_a)$ on the LHS and the RHS of the first equation (we assume that $\overline{M}_a$ is an integer to simplify the discussion).

It follows from Little's result that $\overline{M}_k/M = f_kR_k(M)/R(M)$ and hence $\overline{M}_k = Mkf_k/K_1$. The mean number of locks held per transaction is then

---

[19] The increase in mean response time due to lock contention is similar to its increase in an M/M/1 queueing system discussed in Section 2.3 in Chapter 2, $R = \overline{x}/(1 - \rho)$, with $\overline{x} = r(\overline{M}_a)$ and $\rho = \beta$.

$$\bar{L} = \frac{1}{M} \sum_{k=1}^{K} \bar{L}_k \bar{M}_k \simeq \frac{1}{M} \sum_{k=1}^{K} \frac{k}{2} \bar{M}_k \simeq \frac{1}{2K_1} \sum_{k=1}^{K} k^2 f_k = \frac{K_2}{2K_1}. \qquad (3.8)$$

Consider transactions with the geometric transaction size distribution $f_k = q(1-q)^{k-1}, k \geq 1$ with a mean size $K_1 = 1/q$. Setting $q = 1/k$ such that the size is equal to fixed size transactions of size k. It follows from equation (3.8) that in the case of the geometric distribution $\bar{L} \simeq k$, while $\bar{L} \simeq k/2$ for fixed size transactions, i.e., the P_c in one case is twice that of the other case [ThRy91]. In addition $P_D(2)$ for the geometric distribution is an order of magnitude higher than that for fixed size transactions [ThRy91]. $A = W_1/R(M)$ can be expressed as a function of the first three moments of the number of requested locks (see Appendix B in [ThRy91] and [Thom93b]):

$$A = \frac{W_1}{R(M)} \simeq \frac{K_3 - K_1}{3K_1(K_2 + K_1)}, \qquad (3.9)$$

where the approximation ignores the residual delay in the step in which the lock conflict occurred. It is shown in [Thom93b] that $A \simeq 1$ for the geometric transaction size distribution.

3.1.4 Deadlock Resolution Policies

A comprehensive review of work related to lock conflict and especially dead-lock resolution policies appears in [ACMc87]. The *victim selection* policies considered for resolving deadlocks are based on aborting: (1) the transaction which is the current blocker; (2) a random blocker, i.e., one of the transactions involved in the deadlock cycle; (3) the transaction with the minimum number of locks; (4) the youngest transaction; (5) the transaction which has acquired the minimum amount of processing. It can be concluded from simulation re-sults reported in [ACMc87] that the deadlock resolution method has little effect on the maximum effective throughput (performance differences past the peak throughput are of little interest).

Cyclic restarts occur when restarted transactions have lock conflicts with transactions they have had lock conflict before and these lead to repeated deadlocks, which are resolved by aborting one of the two or more transactions in the deadlock cycle [ACMc87]. Cyclic restarts are possible with policies (1) and (2), while method (4) guarantees that they are prevented. Policies (3) and (5) are pseudo-stable in that they tend to prevent cyclic restarts, but do not guarantee this.

In fact cyclic restarts are more common in the case of some of the restart-oriented locking methods described in Section 4.2 in Chapter 4. *Restart wait-ing* which involves delaying the restart of an aborted transaction, until the conflicting transactions have left the system, prevents cyclic restarts regardless of the victim selection method [RyTh90a],[FrRT92],[Thom96]. This method is applicable to transactions aborted to resolve deadlocks, as well, and is utilized in the simulator in [Thom93b].

Timeouts to resolve deadlocks are more suitable for distributed database systems, where extra messages are required for deadlock detection (see e.g., Section 6.1 in Chapter 6 and Section 8.2 in [CePe84] and [Knap87]). The main shortcoming of this technique is that it is difficult to determine the timeout interval [JeTK89].

3.2 Dynamic Locking and Its Thrashing Behavior

We first analyze the performance of dynamic locking with the general waiting method for the case of identically distributed per step processing times, followed by different per step processing times. Factors contributing to thrashing are next discussed.

3.2.1 Analysis with Identical per Step Processing Times

Consider the case when a transaction is blocked either by an active transaction at level zero (blocking at level one) or a transaction which is blocked by another active transaction (blocking at level two). The probability of being blocked by an active (respectively blocked) transaction is $1 - \beta$ (respectively β) and the mean blocking time in the first case is W_1 and in the second case $1.5W_1$, which can be justified informally as follows. Consider a transaction T_2 which has a lock conflict with a blocked transaction T_1, e.g., $T_2 \to T_1 \to T_0$. T_2 encounters its lock conflict with T_1 at a time distributed uniformly over the time T_1 was blocked by T_0, hence the extra delay for T_1 to be unblocked is $0.5W_1$. T_2 may have been initially blocked by T_1, which became blocked at a later time, resulting in the waits-for graph $T_2 \to T_1 \to T_0$ as before. It can be argued that T_2 had completed one half of its waiting time when T_1 was blocked. More generally, the probability that the effective level of blocking is i is approximated by $P_b(i) = \beta^{i-1}, i > 1$ and $P_b(1) = 1 - \beta - \beta^2 - \beta^3\dots$. The mean waiting time at level $i > 1$ is approximated by $W_i = (i - 0.5)W_1$. The mean overall waiting time (W) is a weighted sum of delays incurred by transactions blocked at different levels

$$W = \sum_{i \geq 1} P_b(i)W_i = W_1 \left[1 - \sum_{i \geq 1} \beta^i + \sum_{i > 1} (i - 0.5)\beta^{i-1} \right]. \tag{3.10}$$

Multiplying both sides by $n_c/R(M)$ and defining $\alpha = n_c W_1/R(M)$ and since $\beta = n_c W/R(M)$ we have

$$\beta = \alpha(1 + 0.5\beta + 1.5\beta^2 + 2.5\beta^3 + \dots). \tag{3.11}$$

It follows that at low lock contention levels $\beta \simeq \alpha$, such that $\overline{M}_a \simeq M(1 - \alpha)$, which corresponds to the lower bound in [TayY87] (see also Section 3.4). This approximation in the form $R(M) = r(M)/(1 - \alpha)$ or $R(\lambda) = r(\lambda)/(1 - \alpha)$ has been used in numerous performance studies. The value for β can be estimated from equation (3.10) by setting $\beta = \alpha$ on the RHS of equation (3.11) [ThRy91].

We can also obtain a closed-form expression for the series by assuming that it is infinite (this is of course more acceptable for larger values of M), since it converges for $\beta < 1$, leading to

$$\beta^3 - (1.5\alpha + 2)\beta^2 + (1.5\alpha + 1)\beta - \alpha = 0. \tag{3.12}$$

It is stated in [TayY90] that "As yet, there are no proposed measures for the resource requirements of a given concurrency control algorithm". Note that α is a single measure, which determines the level of lock contention for standard locking. Two different systems will have the same lock contention level as long as they have the same value for α. It follows from the discussion in Section 3.1 that the value of α for fixed size transactions is one sixth of the α for transactions with a geometric transaction size distribution and the same mean size.

The cubic equation for the dynamic locking system has an algebraic solution (see Appendix B in [Thom93b]), which yields the three roots $0 \le \beta_1 < \beta_1 \le \beta_2 \le 1$ and $\beta_3 \ge 1$ for $\alpha \le \alpha^* = 0.226$ and a single root $\beta_3 > 1$ for $\alpha > \alpha^*$. The value of α^* can be used as an indicator of whether the system is operating in the thrashing region or not. The smallest root β_1 for $\alpha \le \alpha^*$ determines system performance.

The mean number of levels of blocked transactions, excluding active transactions, is given by $\bar{l} = \sum_{i \ge 1} iP_b(i) = (1 - \beta)^{-2} - \beta(1 - \beta)^{-1}$ (corrected expression for $\bar{l}$ in [Thom93b]). At $\beta = 0.378$ which is the thrashing point $\bar{l} \simeq 2$. Also at this point $W/W_1 = \beta/\alpha \simeq 1.7$.

Two cases are possible when the system throughput characteristic $(t(m), m \ge 1)$ is a nondecreasing function which reaches saturation: (i) the system is hardware resource bound, i.e., the system throughput reaches saturation due to hardware resource contention before the system thrashes due to lock contention. There is no reason to increase m further by activating more transactions, once the bottleneck resource is saturated. (ii) The system is lock contention bound and it thrashes before the hardware resource bound is attained. In the latter case the effective throughput ($T(M)$) increases as more transactions are activated and the peak throughput is attained when $\overline{M}_a(= M(1 - \beta))$ is at its maximum. It is observed experimentally, by plotting $\overline{M}_a$ versus β for several distributions for transaction sizes, that $\overline{M}_a$ is maximized at $\beta \simeq 0.3$ [Thom93b]. This is also verified by investigating the maximum value of $\overline{M}_a$ through $d\overline{M}_a/d\alpha = 0$, which yields $\hat{\alpha} = 0.2135$ with a corresponding $\hat{\beta} = 0.296 \simeq 0.3$ [Thom93b]. At this point we have $\bar{l} = 1.6$. and $W \simeq 1.4W_1$. The effective throughput characteristic $(T(M), M \geq 1)$ increases with M, reaches a peak at $\hat{\alpha}$ corresponding to $\hat{M}$ at which $\overline{M}_a$ and hence $T(\hat{M}) \simeq t(0.7\hat{M})$ reach their maximum.

If we subject a system with the effective throughput characteristic $T(M)$, $1 \leq M \leq S$ to quasi-random arrivals with rate $\Lambda(M) = (S - M)/Z$, $1 \leq M \leq S$ (as described in Section 2.1 in Chapter 2), then the intersection point of the two graphs is the equilibrium point of the system, where the transaction arrival rate equals the transaction completion rate. There may be one intersection point in the stable or thrashing region, or three points in which case the system is bistable (refer to the discussion in Section 2.2 in Chapter 2).

The value of $\hat{\alpha}$ can be used for load control. Noting that $\alpha = An_c$, in the case of fixed size transactions $A \simeq 1/3$ and $\hat{n}_c \simeq 0.64$ (as opposed to $\hat{n}_c \simeq 0.75$, which is observed from simulation results in [TaGS85],[TayY87]), while for the geometric distribution $A \simeq 1$ and $\hat{n}_c \simeq 0.21$. Thus by measuring the first three moments of transaction size distribution (K_i, $1 \leq i \leq 3$) yields A, which can be used to estimate $\hat{n}_c$. Also $\hat{P}_c = \hat{n}_c/K_1$, where $\hat{n}_c$ depends on transaction size distribution, can be used as a metric to detect thrashing. Note that this approach is applicable when transaction steps have equal durations.

Another key result from this analysis is that *the variability of transaction size has a major effect on system performance degradation*, e.g., in a system with infinite resources the peak transaction throughput with a (truncated) geometric distribution (considered in [Thom93b]) is approximately a factor of three smaller than the peak throughput with fixed size transactions.

An analysis with limited levels of blocking is also considered in [Thom93b]. We use the framework developed here to show that analyses considering a few levels *cannot predict system behavior at peak performance* and consequently the thrashing point. For example, in a system with two levels of blocking $W = (1 - \beta)W_1 + 1.5\beta W_1$. Noting that $W/W_1 = \beta/\alpha$ and $\nu \triangleq (M - 1)/\alpha \simeq M/\alpha$, after appropriate substitutions we obtain: $\overline{M}_a = M - (2M^2)/(2\nu - M)$. From $d\overline{M}_a/dM = 0$ we obtain $4M^2 - 12\nu M + 4\nu^2 = 0$, which yields $\hat{M} = 0.367\nu$ and $\hat{\beta} = 0.45$, which overestimates the value of β at the peak throughput.

The analysis with the unlimited wait depth is shown to be quite accurate through validation, except at the highest contention level at the extreme points:[20] (i) small M and large k (large transactions); (ii) large M and small k. The problem in the first case is that (i) our analysis is based on mean value arguments that do not hold well for a few transactions; (ii) the analysis does

---

[20] This discussion is also applicable to the case of different processing times for transaction steps.

not take into account the fact that a single transaction may block multiple transactions, i.e., the wait depth is overestimated by our analysis. A detailed analysis to estimate W is reported in [TaGS85],[TayY87], which also considers the case of multiple transactions being enqueued for the same lock (see Figure 11 in [TayY87]). This analysis is of comparable accuracy for medium sized transactions (see Figure 5 in [Thom93b] and also Figure 17 in [TayY87]), but while the analysis in [Thom93b] overestimates performance for small values of k, the analysis in [TayY87] is quite accurate (see Figure 16 in [TayY87]).

3.2.2 Analysis with Different per Step Processing Times

The assumption that transaction steps have identical processing times is relieved here. The mean processing time of the ith step of a transaction in C_k is denoted by $s_k^i(\overline{M}_a)$, $0 \leq i \leq k$, $1 \leq k \leq K$, where $\overline{M}_a$ is the vector of the mean number of active transactions in different classes and steps, which is required to solve the closed queueing network model of the transaction processing system (refer to Section 2.3 in Chapter 2).

The probability of lock conflict with a blocked transaction in the analysis with identical per step processing times is set to β, since active and blocked transactions hold approximately the same number of locks [RyTh90a], but generally when transaction steps have different processing times this probability is given by $\rho \simeq \overline{L}_b/\overline{L}$, where $\overline{L} = \overline{L}_a + \overline{L}_b$ with $\overline{L}_a$ and $\overline{L}_b$ denoting the mean number of locks held by active and blocked transactions, respectively. For example, in the case of incremental static locking, which is a form of dynamic locking where all lock requests are at the beginning of transaction execution (see Section 3.3), ρ is smaller than the case of lock accesses uniformly distributed over the lifetime of a transaction. This is because the time-space of locks held in the active state tends to be high in incremental static locking, since a transaction runs for a long time after acquiring all locks. We have

$$\overline{L}_a = \sum_{k=1}^{K} f_k \sum_{i=1}^{k} \frac{i s_k^i(\overline{M}_a)}{R(M)}, \tag{3.13}$$

$$\overline{L}_b = \sum_{k=1}^{K} f_k \sum_{i=1}^{k} \frac{(i-1)P_c W}{R(M)}. \tag{3.13'}$$

The *conflict ratio*, which is defined as the ratio of the total number of locks held by transactions and the total number of locks held by active transactions [MoWe92], [WHMZ94], is related to ρ as conflict ratio $= 1/(1 - \rho)$ or conversely $\rho = 1 - 1/$conflict ratio.

The probability that a transaction is blocked at level i is then approximated by $P_b(i) = \rho^{i-1}$, $i > 1$ and $P_b(1) = 1 - \rho/(1 - \rho)$. The probability of lock conflict is given by equation (3.1). Similarly to equation (3.5), the mean waiting time with one level of blocking can be approximated by

$$W_1 = \frac{1}{H} \sum_{k=1}^{K} f_k \sum_{i=1}^{k} is_k^i(\overline{M}_a)[\sum_{j=i}^{k} s_k^j(\overline{M}_a) + (k-i)P_cW].$$ (3.14)

The transaction step durations are assumed to be exponentially distributed, but this assumption can be relieved by using the residual lifetime of the step during which the conflict occurred. The normalization constant is $H = \sum_{k=1}^{K} f_k$

$\sum_{i=1}^{k} is_k(\overline{M}_a)$. The term in the brackets is the mean waiting time incurred when a

transaction has a lock conflict with an active transaction in C_k in its ith processing step.

The mean waiting time of a transaction blocked at level i is approximated by $W_i = (i - 0.5)W_1$, $i > 1$, as before. Similarly to equation (3.10) we have

$$W = W_1 (1 + 0.5\rho + 1.5 \, \rho^2 + 2.5\rho^3 + \dots).$$ (3.15)

Since $\rho < 1$, a closed form approximation for the above series can be obtained assuming that it is infinite, we have

$$W = W_1[1 + \frac{\rho(1+\rho)}{2(1-\rho)^2}].$$ (3.16)

Multiplying both sides of the equation by K_1P_c/R we have

$$\beta = \alpha[1 + \frac{0.5\rho(1+\rho)}{(1-\rho)^2}].$$

Note that in addition to α, which determines the level of lock contention in a system with identically distribution transaction steps, a second parameter is required for this purpose when the per step processing times are unequal. To simplify the discussion we assume that the duration of transaction steps are given and are not dependent on $\overline{M}_a$. This obviates the need to compute the mean duration of transaction steps as part of the iterative solution method. The iterative solution method proceeds as follows. Initialize $W = 0$; compute $R(M)$, $\overline{L}_a$, $\overline{L}_b$, and ρ; compute W from equation (3.16). Repeat the iteration until it converges with respect to W (this usually takes a few cycles). The analysis predicts system performance up to the peak throughput quite accurately, but does not converge beyond that point.

Investigations with the numerical solution and simulation results obtained by varying the duration of the last transaction step, which has the most impact on lock holding times, lead to $0.2 < \rho < 0.3$, where the lower (respectively upper) limit is attained when the duration of the last step is very long (respectively equal to others). In fact $\beta \simeq \rho$ in the latter case, since active and blocked transactions hold about the same number of locks in this case (see e.g., [RyTh90a]) [Thom93b]. This range of values of ρ corresponds to 1.25 < conflict ratio < 1.43, which is consistent with results in [MoWe92], [WHMZ94] (also see discussion in Section 3.5). Also similarly to the case of transactions with identical per step processing times, $\overline{M}_a$ is maximized at $\beta \simeq 0.3$. *This provides a very easy to use paradigm for load control*, except in the case of the heterogeneous database access model (see Section 3.5).

3.2.3 Factors Affecting Thrashing

It follows from the analysis that system load for the previous models is determined by $\alpha = K_1 P_c A$ (as well as ρ when the per step processing times are not identical), where P_c increases proportionally to M, the mean number of locks held by transactions, and inversely with the effective database size. The increase in M may be due to the variability inherent in the arrival process, e.g., as noted in Section 2.3 in Chapter 2 the number of requests in an $M/M/1$ queueing system has a geometric distribution. Load control can be applied by setting a multiprogramming level limit $(\overline{M}_{max})$, which can be determined through analysis or simulation for a specific workload. This is unacceptable since the variability in the workload may lead to system underutilization due to thrashing.

One method to reduce the degree of transaction concurrency by reducing transaction residence times in the system is for transactions to incur fewer disk accesses, since disk access times are significantly longer than CPU processing times. This can be partially accomplished through a high hit ratio with respect to the database cache. A main storage database can be utilized to eliminate disk accesses altogether for online transactions [GMSa92], as in the case of IMS Fastpath [GrRe92]. Concurrency control overhead can be reduced in a main storage database by associating extra bits with each object in main storage, which indicates its locking state. In the case of a main storage database it is also advantageous to have a smaller number of faster processors, rather than a larger number of slower processors (with equal overall capacity), since aside from multiprocessing effects (performance degradation due to cache interference and conflicts in storage access), there will be an increase in the system multiprogramming level and hence a higher level of lock contention when slow processors are adopted. Finally, the *effective degree of transaction concurrency* [FrRT92] and the lock contention level can be reduced by adopting one of the two-phase processing methods discussed in Chapter 5.

Analytic and simulation results show that for both models (identical and different per step processing times) the peak performance (the maximum effective throughput) is attained at $\beta \simeq 0.3$, which is an easy to use criterion. Throughput remains flat as we increase the number of transactions in the system, i.e., $\overline{M}_a$ remains the same while the number of blocked transactions increases. It is lock conflicts with blocked transactions which cause the snowball effect leading to thrashing.

The susceptibility of a system to thrashing is affected by the variability of transaction sizes (variability can be defined in other ways, such as the mix of update and read-only transactions). A system with fixed size transactions (with identical per step processing times) may run at the critical value for α^* or even higher values for a long time (i.e., large number of transaction completions) before thrashing occurs, while a system with the geometric distribution for transaction size thrashes for values below α^* [Thom93b].

This phenomenon can be explained as follows. Consider a system with two transaction classes with small and large transactions occurring with equal frequencies ($f_{small} = f_{large} = 0.5$). Let us assume that the system is operating just below its thrashing point for the anticipated load. According to the frequency based model there is a nonzero probability for the system to be subjected to a succession of large transactions, which will lead the system to thrashing. Simulation results in [Thom93b] show that the time to thrashing *decreases* with the increase in variability in transaction size. A by-product of this discussion is that static load control based on a single threshold (say M_{max}) for the number of transactions that can be activated is inadequate.

Temporary variations in the workload, such as an increase in the frequency of accesses to hot spots or the fraction of exclusive lock requests, can possibly lead to thrashing, although of course the probability of this event tends to be very small.[21]

3.3 Performance Analyses of Static Locking

In static locking the identities of all required locks are assumed to be known a priori and the execution of a transaction is started only when all locks have been acquired.

Static locking entails in an increased lock holding time as compared to dynamic locking. The difference in the performance of static and dynamic locking, all other things being equal, depends on the temporal pattern of lock requests over the residence time of a transaction in dynamic locking. Most

---

[21] Generated locking modes according to Bernoulli trials introduces a degree of variability which does not exist in real systems. The effect of locking modes on system performance is discussed further in Section 4.4 in Chapter 4 in the context of wait depth limited methods.

performance studies of dynamic locking postulate that locks are requested uniformly throughout the execution of a transaction, although this is only approximately so, as determined by the analysis of lock traces in [SiSm94]. The performance of the system is obviously affected by the duration of transaction steps as is demonstrated in [TaGS85],[TayY87], which considers incremental static locking, such that locks are requested in quick succession at the beginning of transaction execution. Numerical results in [TaGS85],[TayY87] indicate that dynamic locking outperforms incremental static locking.

In *atomic static locking,* in contrast to incremental static locking, all locks are allocated atomically. The *strict FCFS* and *nonstrict FCFS* transaction scheduling policies for atomic static locking are considered in [ThRy83]. With strict FCFS scheduling transactions are *activated* only in that order, while with nonstrict FCFS scheduling transactions are *considered for activation* in FCFS order, i.e., a transaction is allocated its locks only when they are all available, rather than in piecemeal fashion. Upon the completion of a transaction, the queue of blocked transactions is scanned in FCFS order to activate transactions whose lock requests can be satisfied. A newly arrived transaction can also be activated immediately if its lock requests are satisfied, i.e., it does not have a lock conflict with currently *active* transactions. Otherwise, this transaction is enqueued in FCFS order. The fact that there are no partial allocations of locks to transactions improves performance by precluding unnecessary lock conflicts between newly arriving transactions and blocked transactions. There is a starvation problem associated with the nonstrict FCFS method, in that a transaction requesting a large number of locks may be bypassed repeatedly, which can be fixed by reverting to a strict FCFS method after a transaction has been bypassed too many times. References to static locking in performance evaluation studies without specifying the scheduling method are not uncommon.

Strict FCFS scheduling can be implemented by allowing an arriving transaction to acquire available locks and enqueueing requests for unavailable locks by an atomic action to prevent deadlocks among simultaneously arriving transactions [GaBo83]. The strict FCFS method, unlike the nonstrict method, does not satisfy the *essential blocking* property [FrRo85] (also see Section 4.1 in Chapter 4), that a transaction can only be blocked by a transaction doing "useful work", i.e., an active transaction, which is guaranteed to commit in this case. It is not surprising therefore that a strict FCFS method is outperformed by the latter method as quantified in [ThRy83]. *Strict essential blocking* [FrRT92], differs from essential blocking in that it disallows locks to be acquired before they are actually required. The running priority method (see Section 4.1) partially satisfies the essential blocking property, because locks are requested on demand. The tradeoff between performance and fairness of nonstrict versus strict FCFS method should preferably be resolved in favor of the nonstrict FCFS method, with appropriate safeguards to prevent starvation.

There have been a large number of performance studies of atomic static locking [PoLe80],[GaBo83],[ThRy83],[MoWo85],[Thom85],[TaGS85],[TayY87], [RyTh88]. The analysis in [GaBo83] uses heuristic approximations, which do not lead to accurate results in all cases considered for validation. Next we outline two representative analyses of the nonstrict FCFS method.

A simple analysis of static locking is given in Section 3.7.2 of [TayY87]. A closed system with M transactions is considered, of which $\overline{M}_a$ transactions are active and the remaining transactions are blocked awaiting the release of locks required by them. Given that each transaction requests k locks and the mean transaction processing time is $r = (k + 1)s$, it follows $T(M) = \overline{M}_a/r$ (s is the mean processing time per transaction step, which is set to $1/(k + 1)$ such that $r = 1$ in all cases). A transaction requesting its locks encounters a conflict with probability $p = 1 - (1 - k\overline{M}_a/D)^k$, where $k\overline{M}_a/D$ is the fraction of locks held in the system (note that lock resampling is allowed in this case). Delayed and new transactions request locks with rates a and $T(M)$, respectively, and are unsuccessful in acquiring their locks with probability p, it follows that $a = p(a + T(M))$. Transactions are delayed for $W_b = r/2$ time units, which is the expected time for the conflicting transaction to complete. Noting that $M = \overline{M}_a + aW_b$, it follows that $M = 0.5\overline{M}_a(1 + (1 - k\overline{M}_a/D)^{-k}$, which can be solved to obtain $\overline{M}_a$.

This very simple analysis turns out to be inaccurate in four out of 27 cases considered in [MoWo85], which have high lock contention levels: (i) three cases have a small $M(= 2)$ and large k; (ii) one case has a large M and small $k(= 2)$. Mean value arguments used in the analysis do not hold for small values for M, while for small k multiple transactions are possibly blocked by the same lock, which results in their serial execution. This effect is usually not taken into account in the analyses of dynamic locking, as noted in Section 3.2. This analysis is extended in [ThRy89] which allows different distributions for transaction processing time, multiple transaction classes, shared and exclusive lock requests, and query and update transactions. The validation study in [ThRy89] showed this method to be acceptably accurate, except in the extreme cases defined above.

One of the first analysis of static locking utilizes the decomposition method to represent the computer system by a flow-equivalent service center (see Section 2.3.6 in Chapter 2) and a Markov chain with a large number of states at the higher level [PoLe80]. It is assumed that "transaction accesses are uniformly distributed over the cells of the database", but this assumption is not reflected in the analysis (see discussion in Section 2.2 in Chapter 2). This work however motivated the analyses in [ThRy83] and [MoWo85]. In what follows we present the analysis of atomic static locking with exclusive lock requests according to [RyTh88], which uses recursive equations replacing the nested summations given in [ThRy83] (see Section 3.3). The derivation of the recursive equations can be explained easily and they provide an efficient computational method to derive numerical results. Sequential granule placement, in addition to random granule placement, is considered in [RyTh88] (see Section 2.2 in Chapter 2).

The analysis is presented in top-down manner by expressing the performance measure of interest, in this case the effective throughput, as a function of other variables, whose value is not known a priori. The process is repeated until all variables are expressed as functions of input variables and each other. It turns out that a noniterative solution is possible in this case, but this is usually not the case in analyzing concurrency control methods, see e.g., [RyTh87],[RyTh90b],[Thom93b],[Thom94a],[Thom95c].

The effective throughput is given by $T(M) = \sum_{J=1}^{M} \pi(J) t(J)$, where the system throughput characteristic ($t(J)$, $1 \leq J \leq M$) can be computed using the methods described in Section 2.3 in Chapter 2. The steady-state probability or the fraction of time that there are J active transactions in the system is denoted by $\pi(J)$, which can be obtained by solving a Markov chain whose states are S_J, $1 \leq J \leq M$. The transitions among the states are computed below based on the number of transactions activated upon the completion of a transaction. The state equilibrium equations for the Markov chain are given as follows

$$\pi(J)t(J) = \sum_{l=1}^{J} \pi(J)P_t(J,l)t(J), \quad 1 \leq J \leq M. \tag{3.17}$$

Note that $\pi(0) = 0$, since at least one transaction is active. The steady-state probabilities $\pi(J), 1 \leq j \leq M$ can be obtained by solving the set of linear equations plus the normalizing equation ($\sum_{J=1}^{M} \pi(J) = 1$). The state transition probabilities $P_t(J,l) = Pr[S_J \rightarrow S_l]$ for $1 \leq l \leq M$ and $1 \leq J \leq M$ are derived below.

The following three steps occur when a transaction completes at S_J.

1. A state transition $S_J \rightarrow S_{J-1}$, if no other transactions are activated, otherwise it is just a transient state transition, since the time for transaction scheduling is ignored.

2. The $M - J$ blocked transactions are considered for activation in FCFS order and there is a transition to $J - 1 + k$ if $1 \leq k \leq M - J$ transactions are activated.

Let $P_a(I, b, J)$ denote the probability that the (possibly temporary) transition $S_J \rightarrow S_I$ occurs after b transactions are considered for activation. Then $P[S_{J-1} \rightarrow S_{J-1+k}] = P_a(J - 1 + k, M - J, J)$.

The probability that a blocked transaction is unblocked following b other transactions upon a completion at S_J is denoted by $P_r(b, J)$

3. The new transaction replacing the completed transaction is considered for activation after the $M - J$ blocked transactions. The probability that it can be activated immediately when there are J active transactions in the system is denoted by $P_s(J)$.

The probabilities $P_a(I,b,J)$ can be computed using the following recursive equations for $1 \le b \le M - J$ and $J - 1 \le I \le M - 1$

$$P_a(I, b,J) = P_a(I, b - 1,J)[1 - P_r(0,J)], \quad I = J - 1, \qquad (3.18)$$

$$P_a(I, b,J) = P_a(I, b - 1,J)[1 - P_r(I - J + 1,J)] +$$

$$P_a(I - 1, b - 1,J)P_r(I - J + 1,J), \quad I > J - 1.$$

where $P_a(I, 0,J) = 1$ for $I = J - 1$ and zero otherwise. The first (respectively second) term in the second equation corresponds to a transaction unblocking (respectively a transaction remaining to be blocked). As far as the newly introduced transaction is concerned, we have

$$P_a(I, M - J,J) = P_a(I, M - J + 1,J)[1 - P_s(I)], \quad I = J - 1. \qquad (3.19)$$

$$P_a(I, M - J,J) = P_a(I, M - J + 1,J)[1 - P_s(I)] +$$

$$P_a(I - 1, M - J + 1,J)P_s(I), \quad I > J - 1.$$

The transition probabilities for the state equilibrium equations are given by $1 \le J \le M$ and $J - 1 \le I \le M$ as follows

$$P_t(J,I) = P_a(I, M - J + 1, J). \qquad (3.20)$$

A new transaction does not have a history of lock conflicts with previously active and recently activated transactions. Given that there are J active transactions in the system, we have

$$P_s(J) = \binom{D - J \times k}{k} / \binom{D}{k}. \qquad (3.21)$$

As far as previously blocked transactions are concerned, let $P_c(J)$ denote the probability that the transaction has been waiting for the just completed transaction, or upon a completion at S_J the blocked transaction does *not* have a lock conflict with the *remaining* $J - 1$ transactions, given that it had a lock conflict with one of the J active transactions. Note that $P_c(J) = 1$ - Prob[target transaction does have a lock conflict with the remaining $J-1$ transactions| target transaction did have a lock conflict with the active J transactions], hence

$$P_c(J) = 1 - \frac{1 - P_s(J - 1)}{1 - P_s(J)}. \tag{3.22}$$

Let $P_o(b,J)$ denote the probability that a transaction does not have a lock conflict with $J+b-1$ transactions, given that it did not have a conflict with the remaining $J-1$ transactions.

$$P_o(b,J) = \frac{Pr[\text{No conflict with } J+b-1 \text{ transactions}]}{Pr[\text{No conflict with } J-1 \text{ transactions}]} =$$

$$\binom{D - (J + b - 1)k}{k} \Big/ \binom{D - (J - 1)k}{k}. \tag{3.23}$$

It follows that $P_r(b, J) = P_c(J)P_o(b, J)$. This completes the analysis, since all unknown variables have been expressed as functions of input parameters.

Validation results show this analysis to be quite accurate [RyTh88], which is also true for the analysis in [MoWo85]). Thus a relatively simple probabilistic analysis can be used for evaluating the performance of static locking, which does not require the assumptions made in [TayY87],[ThRy89]. An extension of this analysis to take into account nonexclusive lock requests appears in [MoWo84].

In a system with infinite resources the throughput for atomic static locking with a nonstrict FCFS method increases monotonically as more transactions become available for scheduling (the system throughput characteristic is assumed to be a monotonically nondecreasing function of M and scheduling overhead is ignored). This is because locks are not held unnecessarily and there is no wasted processing due to scheduling overhead. As more and more transactions become available, the rate of increase in the number of active transactions diminishes, i.e., the effective throughput characteristic reaches an asymptotic value. In theory, the maximum number of transactions that can be activated in the system with an infinite backlog of transactions with a nonstrict FCFS scheduler is floor(D/k), i.e., when almost all the locks in the database are utilized! Numerical results in [TayY87],[ThRy86] show that dynamic locking initially outperforms static locking, which is due to the shorter lock holding times and lower lock contention level, allowing higher degrees of transaction concurrency, but that it is outperformed by static locking after the onset of thrashing (see e.g., Figure 32 in [TayY87]).

3.4 Performance Analyses of Dynamic Locking

Surveys of analytic solutions for dynamic locking also appear in [TayY87],[RyTh90a],[ThRy91],[Thom93b]. In Sections 3.1 and 3.2 we described an analytic solution method for dynamic locking, which was based on mean value analysis [Thom93b] . This section gives an overview of various methods applicable to the analysis of standard locking. Unless otherwise specified a closed system with M fixed size transactions of size k is considered.

- Analytic solutions based on queueing network models extend the hardware resource contention model to incorporate lock contention [IrLi79],[Thom82]. A central-server model as described in Section 2.3.1 in Chapter 2 is utilized to represent hardware resource contention and D pseudo-servers to represent the lock contention delays for the D database locks. Both studies use *job class switching* [Lave83], rather than probabilistic routing, to ensure that the number of cycles made by transactions in the central-server model, as well as the number of lock requests, is fixed, rather than geometrically distributed (refer to Section 2.3 in Chapter 2).[22]

The pseudo-servers are only visited when there is a lock conflict and they are modeled as delay servers (see Section 2.3 in Chapter 2). The delay at the nodes is the mean waiting time (W), which is not known a priori, but can be expressed as a function of the mean transaction residence time (R). Thus $W = R$ is used in [IrLi79] and $W = R/2$ in [Thom82]. It follows from the analysis in [TayY87],[TayY90] that $R/2$ is the average of the light and heavy load (lock contention) waiting times, which are shown to be $R/3$ and $2R/3$ (note that the heavy load mean waiting time in this case is higher than that obtained by the analysis in Section 3.2.1). The fact that the pseudo-servers are delay servers, allows them to be *aggregated* by adding their service demands to yield a single delay server with $X_{lock-delay} = P_c W$ (the contention for each lock is P_c/D and there are D delay servers).

The analysis in [Thom82] considers D FCFS servers to model the waiting time for lock acquisition. From the viewpoint of numerical results, FCFS servers lead to the same results as delay servers, because the utilization of individual locks is very low. From the modeling viewpoint delay servers are more appropriate, since W includes queueing delays in this case. The symmetry due to uniform accesses to database objects results in a subnetwork of balanced servers which can be easily aggregated into a single aggregate server (see Section 2.3.5 in Chapter 2).

The analyses in [ThRy91],[Thom93b] uses the analysis in Sections 3.1 and 3.2 to estimate W, which is the mean time spent at the delay server per lock conflict. The analysis in [Thom82] thus emphasizes the solution of the queueing network model, while the analysis in [ThRy91],[Thom93b] emphasize the lock contention model (with the queueing network model solved as part of a background computation [Lave83],[LZGS84]).

---

[22] The detailed representation of job class switching as in the analysis in [IrLi79],[Thom82] is not required, but has been provided in both papers for tutorial purposes. Given that the service demand of the ith step of a transaction at device n is $X_{n,i}$, while the total service demand is X_n, yields the mean time spent in step i at device n as $r_{n,i} = (X_{n,i}/X_n)r_n$.

- The analytic solution method in [TaGS85],[TayY87] is based on *flow diagrams,* which are described in detail in Section 4.5 of Chapter 4. Referring to Figure 4.1 in Chapter 4, the states in the first row correspond to active states and states in the second row correspond to blocked states. Deadlocks are ignored, hence transaction aborts represented by transitions to the initial state do not occur, until the transaction is completed. Due to the fact that the probability of lock conflict (P_c) remains constant as transactions make progress, the steady-state probabilities for all active states are equal and the same is true for blocked states (these steady-state probabilities are derived in Section 4.5.3 in Chapter 4). The most difficult aspect of the analysis is estimating W, which is accomplished by making several assumptions about the waits-for graph. The analysis leads to a cubic equation for the dynamic locking system in $\overline{M}_a$, with three roots in the intervals $(-\infty, M(1 - k^2\Lambda/3)$, $(M(1 - k^2\Lambda/3),(M(1 - k^2\Lambda/6))$, and $(M(1 - k^2\Lambda/3), +\infty)$, for $k^2\Lambda < 1.5$ where $\Lambda = M/D$. The second root is the only one of interest. Note the similarity of these expressions to $\overline{M}_a = M(1 - \beta)$.

  The term inside the parentheses can be expressed as $k^2\Lambda/F \simeq P_c W/R$, where F specifies the denominator (3 or 6) in the previous expressions and P_c is given by equation (3.1). For the upper (respectively lower) bound $W/R = 1/3$ (respectively $= 2/3$), with an arithmetic mean $W/R = 1/2$ (rather than 1/2.25 in author's earlier works as corrected in [TayY90]), which coincides with the approximation used in [Thom82].

- The analysis in Section B in [ThRy91] allows variable transaction sizes and different processing times for transaction steps, which are obtained from an underlying queueing network model. Only two levels of transaction blocking with currently active transactions and transactions which are blocked by active transactions are considered. Simulation results show that this analysis is quite accurate up to relatively high lock contention levels, but cannot predict peak throughput. A similar analysis is also presented in [YuDL93].

- An analytic solution based on a Markov chain representing the state of the system appears in [RyTh90a], which is influenced by the analysis in [ThRy83]. At the lower level of the model we consider a closed system with a fixed number of transactions (M). The system state is represented simply by the number of active transactions ($1 \leq J \leq M$). The holding time in each state is determined by an underlying computer system model. Transitions occur on a per transaction step basis, i.e., at the completion of a step a transaction requests a new lock or commits. A lock request may result in the transition $J \rightarrow J$, $J \rightarrow J - 1$, and $J \rightarrow I$, $I \geq J$ depending on whether the lock request is successful, unsuccessful with blocking, and unsuccessful with an abort (the locks released by an aborted transaction may result in the activation of other transactions). A multilevel solution method is adopted, which facilitates bottom-up validation (see Section 2.4 in Chapter

2) and modifications to some levels of analysis without affecting others, e.g., a different lock conflict model can be adopted. The solution method is also based on very few approximations and takes into account deadlocks, while this is not the case for the other solution methods for dynamic locking [TaGS85],[ThRy91],[Thom93b].

An iterative solution method based on the equilibrium point analysis [Tasa86], which is described in Section 2.3 in Chapter 2 is also applicable in this case. Given that $P_t(J,I)$ denotes the transition rate from S_J to S_I, the equilibrium state S_{J^*} and hence the mean number of active transactions $\bar{J} = J^*$ can be determined by solving

$$A(J) = \sum_{I=J-1}^{M} (I - J)P_t(J,I) = 0.$$

The number of unblocked transactions decreases as J increases, hence $A(J)$ is a monotonically decreasing function in J (this was also verified numerically). The value of J^* can be determined from the above equation using the bisection method in $\log_2(M)$ steps.

3.4.1 Analysis with Shared and Exclusive Locks and Nonuniform Database Accesses

The *effective database size paradigm* provides an elegant approach for dealing with shared and exclusive lock requests and nonuniform database accesses in the case of the general waiting method [TaGS85],[TayY87]. Shared and exclusive lock requests to a database of size D can be substituted with exclusive lock requests only to a database of size $D_{eff} = D/[1 - (1 - f_x)^2]$, where f_x denotes the fraction of exclusive lock requests (a similar expression is obtained in [Mitr85],[Lave84], see Section 2.4). To show that this is so let $\bar{N}_x$ and $\bar{N}_s$ denote the mean number of objects locked in shared and exclusive mode, respectively. Since multiple transactions may hold a lock on the same object, then the number of shared locks in the system is $\bar{N}'_s \geq \bar{N}_s$, while $\bar{N}'_x = \bar{N}_x$ for the number of exclusive locks. The total number of locks held in the system is $\bar{N}' = \bar{N}'_x + \bar{N}'_s$ then $\bar{N}'_x = f_x\bar{N}'$ and $\bar{N}'_s = (1 - f_x)\bar{N}'$. The mean number of objects locked in shared mode is related to the number of shared locks held in the system by

$$\bar{N}_s = D[1 - (1 - 1/D)^{\bar{N}'_s}] \simeq \bar{N}'_s, \tag{3.24}$$

where the approximation is due to the fact that D is much larger than $\bar{N}'_s$. It follows from the previous discussion that $\bar{N}_x \simeq f\bar{N}'$ and $\bar{N}_s \simeq (1 - f)\bar{N}'$. Let $\bar{N} = \bar{N}_x + \bar{N}_s$ denote the mean number of objects locked in the system, it follows that $\bar{N}_x \simeq f_x\bar{N}$ and $\bar{N}_s \simeq (1 - f_x)\bar{N}$. The probability of lock conflict is a weighted sum of the probabilities of lock conflict when the lock request is in exclusive and shared mode:

$$P_c \simeq f_X \frac{\overline{N}_X + \overline{N}_S}{D} + (1 - f_X) \frac{\overline{N}_X}{D} \simeq \frac{(2f_X - f_X^2)\overline{N}}{D} = \frac{\overline{N}}{D_{eff}}, \qquad (3.25)$$

where the last equality follows from the aforementioned expression for D_{eff}. Note that this result also concurs with [Lave84] (refer to Chapter 1). It is shown in [TaGS85],[TayY87] that this transformation also applies to W.

In the case of the nonuniform database access model, where a fraction b of database accesses are to a fraction c of the database, it is shown in [TaGS85],[TayY87] that $D_{eff} = D/[b^2/c + (1 - b)^2/(1 - c)]$, where the denominator can be expressed as $1 + (b - c)^2/c(1 - c)$.

In the case of shared and exclusive lock requests the validation of equation (3.25) in [TayY87] is limited to $f_X = 0.5$, in which case the effective database size paradigm provides an accurate estimate of system throughput. Further validations with smaller values of f_X, more typical for transaction processing workloads, are desirable. At heavier loads the approximation in equation (3.24) may not hold, since there may be multiple transactions holding a shared lock. This also affects the calculation of W, because it is more likely that a transaction requesting an exclusive lock becomes blocked by multiple transactions holding shared locks, i.e., its mean waiting time is the *expected value of the maximum* of several lock holding times in shared mode.

An improvement in performance in the case of shared and exclusive locks is possible by reducing lock utilization in shared mode by adopting a non-FCFS method, such that shared locks can bypass exclusive locks if the lock is already held in shared mode. A threshold method may be used for exclusive locks, such that new shared lock requests are blocked when the number of exclusive lock requests for the object exceeds a certain threshold, say $K_{X-threshold}$. Timeout intervals instead or in addition to the threshold method can be used to prevent long delays for exclusive lock requests. Lock utilization in shared mode decreases with $K_{X-threshold}$, due to the increased degree of concurrency in processing shared locks. It is shown in [ThNi93] that a threshold method (without timeouts) outperforms the FCFS method, i.e., achieves a higher throughout, which is simply because shared locks are served at a higher degree of concurrency than the FCFS method.

The effective database size paradigm in the context of restart-oriented locking methods is discussed in Section 4.4 in Chapter 4.

3.5 On More Realistic Modeling of Lock Contention

Most performance studies of concurrency control methods are concerned with a *homogeneous database access model*, i.e., transaction accesses to the database are not distinguishable from each other. A minor variation from this model is the distinction made between update and query transactions, where the latter only request locks in shared mode [TayY87].

More realistic models of transaction processing are described in [JeTK89],[Thom94a],[Thom95c], where [JeTK89] is a simulation study of a forerunner of the TPC-C benchmark [Gray93] in a shared-nothing system. In this section we describe the model in [Thom94a] and outline the conclusions of a simulation study for load control. A suggestion for an even more realistic model based on the most common execution sequences of transactions is additionally provided. We then list some extensions to the locking model.

3.5.1 Heterogeneous Database Access Model

Consider a closed system with M transactions in J classes accessing I database regions (the ith database region is denoted by DBR_i). According to the frequency based model the fraction of transactions processed in C_j is $f_j, 1 \leq j \leq J$. Transactions in C_j access DBR_i in their nth step with probability $g_{j,n,i}$. This can be represented by a bypartite graph, where one set of nodes represents transaction steps and the other set the $DBRs$. The weight of the link from node for the nth step of a transaction in C_j (say $C_{j,n}$) to DBR_i is $g_{j,n,i}$, i.e., $C_{j,n} \overset{g_{j,n,i}}{\rightarrow} DBR_i$.

To motivate the necessity for the proposed database model, consider a closed system with transactions requesting $K = 16$ exclusive locks, while there are in fact two transactions classes with equal frequencies ($f_1 = f_2 = 0.5$) each requesting 16 locks, such that locks requested by C_1 (respectively C_2) are from DBR_1 (respectively DBR_2) with $D_1 = 4096$ (respectively $D_2 = 16384$) objects. The simulation yields $P_c = 0.00554$ at $M = 10$. An observer who only knows that transactions request sixteen locks, may assume that lock requests are uniform with respect to the objects in the database and that lock request instants are uniform over the lifetime of a transaction (transaction steps with equal durations), i.e., $\bar{L} \simeq K/2 = 8$, which leads to $D_{eff} \simeq (M-1)\bar{L}/P_c \simeq 13000$. The observer using D_{eff} in another simulation experiment with $M = 50$ obtains $T'(50) = 235.5$, while the original simulator yields $T(50) = 202$ for its peak throughput, i.e., the throughput is overestimated by 16.5%. Monitoring database accesses would yield $b \simeq 0.50$ and $c \simeq 4096/20480 = 0.20$, from which [TaGS85],[TayY87] $D_{eff} = D/[b^2/c + (1-b)^2/(1-c)] = 15059$. The hot-spot model is a good predictor of system performance if the fractions $f_1 = f_2 = 0.5$ are maintained as M is varied, but can be inaccurate otherwise.

The analytic solution method in Sections 3.1 and 3.2 (with different processing times for transaction steps) is extended in [Thom94a],[Thom95c] to this model and shown to be acceptably accurate in predicting system performance up to very high levels of lock contention, but not necessarily peak throughput.

Simulation studies to gain insight into the issue of load control for this model lead to the following conclusions:

1. Transactions in the system may belong to two disjoint sets from the viewpoint of the database regions being accessed. Transactions in one set have a high level of lock contention, while the transactions in the other set do not. The thrashing of transactions in the first set leads the whole system to thrash because of the frequency based model, since completed transactions in set 2 are gradually replaced by transactions in set 1, since they stay much longer in the system. Higher values for β and ρ are indicators of thrashing, but their critical value varies with system parameters (a rather limited range of conflict ratios was observed in [WHMZ94]).

   In case the number of transactions in the two sets executed in two regions with multiprogramming levels M_1 and M_2 with $M_1 + M_2 = M$ then the transactions in the second region will not be affected by the fact that transactions in the other region are thrashing. The overall values of β and ρ are not good indicators of the occurrence of thrashing in this case.

   Conversely the fraction of blocked transactions in C_j (β_j) may be quite high, without leading to thrashing, when $\overline{M}_j$ is rather small.

2. The value of ρ (as defined in Section 3.2) varies in the range (0.211-0.376) in one experiment and (0.245-0.376) in another. Conflict ratios are observed to be in the range (1.26-1.60) based on the experimental results reported in [WHMZ94], which is consistent with these figures (note that the conflict ratio equals $(1 - \rho)^{-1}$).

   In spite of the concurrence of these results, there is no guarantee that these values of ρ or the conflict ratio will hold in other systems.

Load control based on the composition of transactions in the system seems to be the only feasible approach in this case [Thom94a],[Thom95c]. Consider a system with two (interfering) transaction classes and assume that the maximum throughput attained in the two classes is $T_1(\hat{M}_1, 0)$ and $T_2(0, \hat{M}_2)$. Let us assume that the system is guaranteed to run $T'_1(., .)$ ($< T_1(\hat{M}_1, 0)$) transactions in C_1 per second. A table-driven method can be used for load control by providing $T_i(M_1, M_2)$, $i = 1,2$ for various compositions of transaction classes. This table can be used to determine the multiprogramming level limit for transactions in C_2 to guarantee $T'_1(.,.)$, when this throughput is being exceeded. This method is more flexible than the one discussed in [WHMZ94], which sets multiprogramming level limits on transaction classes and their combinations by adding one transaction class at a time to the transaction mix.[23] The problem with applying the table based approach is the difficulty of generating the table

---

[23] The example in [WHMZ94] considers a system with three transaction classes with multiprogramming level limits 35, 20, and 15 for transactions in C_1, C_2, and C_3, respectively. The multiprogramming level limit for C_1 plus C_2 is 40, and it is 35 over all classes. The number of transactions allocated in the system should satisfy all the constraints, e.g., the number of transactions in C_1 is 35 when there are no other transaction classes, its 30 when there

in a system with a large number of transaction classes. On the other hand, firstly, the number of dominant transaction classes in a system may be rather small, and secondly, it may be possible to aggregate several transaction classes into one class to reduce the number of classes to be considered. This remains an area of further investigation.

Schedulers for transaction processing systems take into account several factors, mainly based on transaction response time objectives, but also to control the lock contention level. Our discussion of the IMS transaction scheduler is quite brief. An IMS transaction has a *type* and multiple transaction types may belong to a *class*. Transaction classes are assigned to *"message" processing regions,* such that each region can process several transaction classes and a transaction class may be processible in several regions. There may be a different processor priority associated with each class in a region [IBMC94].

The level of lock contention in the system is affected by the assignment process, e.g., by setting a limit on the number of transactions in the same class. Manipulation of locking traces, e.g., through "folding" which superimposes lock requests from nonoverlapping time periods to achieve a higher throughput, may contradict with the reduction in lock contention introduced by transaction scheduling. An analytic solution for the queueing network model of IMS transaction processing systems, which takes into account the above complications, but not lock contention, is given in [Serr84]. This solution method is a specialized case of open queueing network models with population size constraints [ThBa84] (see Section 2.3.4).

3.5.2 Characterization of Transaction Workloads

Transactions in the same transaction class may have a different execution sequence based on their input data and the state of the database. For example, 98% of debit transactions are processed normally, while 2% result in an overdraft requiring additional processing, e.g., to check credit limits, etc. This case can be specified by two subclasses with respective frequencies. These subclasses may correspond to fixed size transactions with deterministic database accesses, i.e., $g_{j,n,i} = 1$. More complex transactions may not lend themselves to a static classification into subclasses and the monitoring of transaction executions is required for this purpose.

In effect, the transaction is characterized by a finite-state machine, with an initial state (beginning of transaction-BOT) and one or multiple end of transaction-EOT states. The state transition probabilities among the states correspond to a first-order Markov chain [Klei75],[Koba81]. The number of

---

are 10 transactions in C_2, and its only 10 when there are 10 transactions in C_2 and 15 transactions in C_3.

transaction subclasses is determined by all possible paths from the initial to the final state(s) of the transaction, which may be quite large, even if there are no cycles. The mean number of visits to the states of the Markov chain [Klei75] can be used to estimate the number of locks required in various database regions. The average lock holding time (for a subclass) can be obtained through measurement or by summing the duration of the states throughout which a lock is held. The analysis of lock contention can then proceed by extending the heterogeneous database access model.

Parameters for existing transactions can be obtained through measurements on operational systems. The viability of this model can be ascertained by its ability to validate against measurement results for the baseline system. The model can then be used in predictive studies, using roughly estimated parameters for new transaction classes (by inspecting the associated code). A comprehensive discussion of workload characterization appears in [FeSZ83]. The discussion in [WeZo86], which deals with characterizing the future access patterns of canned transactions for data prefetching purposes, is also relevant to this discussion.

3.5.3 Other Extensions to Lock Contention Models

We consider relational databases in this discussion, although hierarchical DBMSs (such as IMS) and network DBMSs are heavily used in legacy systems.

- A more extended set of lock request modes, including multigranularity locking, intent locks, and cursor locks need be considered [Date83], [GrRe92] (see Section 3.7).

  The analysis or simulation of standard locking with a given lock compatibility matrix (as given in Section 3.7) requires a better characterization of lock request patterns, which would provide more insights into the locking behavior of transaction processing systems.

- Distinguishing locks intended for indexes versus data blocks. This is because indexes may constitute hot-spots and a database which normally provides page level locking, may allow locking at the level of fractions of pages for indexes to relieve lock contention [IBMC95] (see Section 3.7).

  In fact a large number of specialized locking methods have been developed for operations on index structures, which entail in a short lock holding time, while providing for recovery [MoLe92],[Moha95].

  Performance evaluation of concurrency control methods for index structures, such as B+ trees has been an area of much activity by itself. A survey of previous work and a simulation study for this purpose appears in [SrCa93]. Analytic methods to compare the performance of several schemes for operating on B* trees are presented in [JoSh93].

- It is postulated in most studies that transactions request one lock at a time ([Reut95] is an exception). For example, multiple records residing on different database blocks may be "selected" by a SQL statement issued by a transaction. A subset of the lock requests may be unsuccessful and the transaction may only proceed after all locks are acquired.

- Most performance studies of concurrency control methods postulate data accesses uniformly distributed over a database whose size (D) is given. In fact only a subset of database objects are accessed at any one time, usually with nonuniform probabilities [SiSm94]. When only the probability of lock conflict (P_c) is available, then D can be estimated from equation (3.1), or equation (3.25) if there are shared as well as exclusive lock requests.

Another major weakness of performance evaluation studies of locking methods, in particular, and concurrency control methods, in general, is the *fixed database size assumption*, i.e., the database size D is assumed to be fixed as the number of activated transactions M varies. This is not so for some applications, such as the debit-credit transactions in banking, as exemplified by the TPC-A or TPC-B benchmarks [Gray93], where the number of records increases proportionally with the number of bank clients. In some applications a certain table size may remain fixed, while the sizes of other tables varies with the workload [Thom94a],[Thom95c]. For example, the number of suppliers in an order entry application, such as the TPC-C benchmark [Gray93] may increase much more slowly than the number of customers.

3.6 Miscellaneous Transaction Models

The concurrent processing of long read-only queries for decision support applications and short update transactions may introduce very high lock conflict levels between the two workloads if certain precautions are not taken (conflicts among update transactions are not considered at this point). A long-running query with a strict two-phase locking paradigm which locks a significant fraction of the objects of the database in shared mode for relatively long periods of time cannot be tolerated in an online transaction processing environment. One method to allow such concurrent processing is to reduce the level of consistency for queries by running queries at level 1 or 2 consistency, i.e., reading uncommitted data or obtaining locks only for the duration of a read [Date83],[GrRe92]. The latter ensures "cursor stability", but does not guarantee "repeatable reads", which requires shared locks with strict two-phase locking [Date83]. There is a significant degree of contention between cursor locks and exclusive locks [SiSm94], which results in a slowdown of query processing and wasting system resources, such as buffer space.

Versioning methods provide another alternative. A large number of versioning methods have been proposed, which are reviewed in [BoCa92],[MoPL92]. Multiversion concurrency control theory is given in [BeHG87]. The simulation study in [BoCa92] shows that versioning (at the record rather than page level) can be used to allow improved query processing, while [MoPL92] presents a *transient* versioning method with many desirable features, which can be incorporated into the framework of the ARIES recovery method [MHL+92].

The concept of *nested transactions* [Moss85] (also see Section 4.7 in [GrRe92]) offers "more decomposable execution units and finer grained control over concurrency and recovery than flat transactions". Furthermore, it supports the decomposition of "unit of work" into subtasks and their appropriate distribution in a computer system, which is a prerequisite of intratransaction parallelism [HaRo93]. Multilevel transactions [Weik91] (also see Section 4.9 in [GrRe92]) are related to nested transactions, but are more specialized. For example, transactions hold long term record level locks (more generally object level locks [WeHa93]), while page level locks are held by subtransactions for the duration of operations on records. *Compensating operations* for subtransactions are provided for rollback. An implementation of multilevel transactions and a performance evaluation using synthetic benchmarks is reported in [WeHa93].

Ordered sharing allows a flexible lock compatibility matrix, as long as operations are executed in the same order as locks are acquired [AEAL94]. Thus it introduces restrictions on the manner transactions are written. For example, a transaction T_2 may obtain a shared lock on an object locked in exclusive mode by T_1, i.e., read the value written by T_1, but this will result in deferring T_1's commit, to after T_2 is committed. Simulation results in [AEAL94] show that there is an improvement in performance with respect to standard locking, which can be ascribed to the fact that transaction waiting time has been reduced with respect to standard locking.

Altruistic locking allows transactions to *donate* previously locked object, once they are done with them, but before the object is actually unlocked at transaction completion time [SGMS94]. Another transaction may lock a donated object, but to ensure serializability, it should remain in the "wake" of the original transaction, i.e., accesses to objects should be ordered. Cascading aborts which are a possibility when the donated object was locked in exclusive mode can be prevented by restricting "donations" to objects held in shared mode only. This makes the approach more suitable for read-only queries or long-running transactions with few updates.

The synchronization technique and scheduling method described in [Baye86] is similar and allows simultaneous processing of a batch transaction and short (possibly update) transactions (at consistency level 3). *Random batch transactions* update database records only once (converting them from old to new records) and the updates are independent of the order in which they are carried out. There is a conflict if a short transaction needs to access old and new records. Since the blocking delay is not tolerable for short transactions, the batch transaction may update the *required* old records and make them available to short transactions after taking *intermediate commit-points* [Date83],[Baye86].

The *proclamation-based* model for cooperating transactions is described in [JaSh92]. In addition to its original motivation of transaction cooperation, it can be used to reduce the level of lock contention. This method is different from altruistic locking in that a transaction instead of releasing its lock on an object that it is not going to modify again, proclaims one or a set of possible values for it which can be accessed by other transactions. Transactions interested in the object can proceed with their execution according to the proclaimed value(s). Note that this method has similarities to the polyvalues method in [Mont78] (see Section 5.4 in Chapter 5).

The *escrow method* [ONei86] is a generalization of the field calls approach in IMS Fastpath [GrRe92] (see also discussion of polyvalues in Section 5.1 in Chapter 5), where the minimum, current, and maximum values of an aggregate variable are made available to other transactions. Let us assume that a banking account with a current balance of $1000, has a credit transaction for $100 and a debit transaction for $200 in progress. Then the balance is represented by ($800,$1000,$1100). The final balance is $900 if both transactions are successful, but a debit transaction for $500 need not be delayed for either or both transactions to complete or abort, since there are adequate funds in the account in all cases.

Lock holding time by long-lived transactions can be reduced by using intermediate commit points according to the *sagas paradigm* [GMSa87] (see also Section 4.11.3 in [GrRe92]). A long-lived transaction T is viewed as a set of subtransactions $T_1, ..., T_n$, which are executed sequentially and can be committed individually at their completion. However, the abort of subtransaction T_j results in the undoing of the updates of all preceding subtransactions *from a semantic point of view* through *compensating subtransactions* $C_1, ...C_{j-1}$. Compensating transactions consult the log to determine the parameters to be used in compensation.

A method for *chopping transactions* into smaller transactions to reduce the level of lock contention and increase concurrency, while preserving correctness, is presented in [SLSP95]. Preserving correctness requires knowledge about the set of transactions that are running concurrently with the transaction to be chopped. Examples of correct and incorrect "choppings" are given in [SLSP95] and will not be repeated here, but it suffices to say that subtransactions should be executed in a certain order and critical steps which may fail should be executed first.

That smaller transactions result in a lower level of lock contention can be justified by the following example. Let us assume that M transactions requesting k locks can be substituted by $2M$ transactions each requesting $k/2$ locks from a database with D objects. Then the probability that a transaction encounters a lock conflict in the first case is $P_w \simeq kP_c \simeq (M-1)k^2/(2D)$ while in the second case it is $P_w \simeq k/2P_c \simeq (2M-1)k^2/(8D)$, which is approximately half of the previous value. Simulation results in [SLSP95] show a significant improvement in performance when a long running transaction (say a batch update) is chopped into smaller transactions, but this is at the cost of an increased number of commits. Other works related to transaction chopping are reviewed in [SLSP95] and will not be repeated here.

Semantics-based concurrency control methods rely upon the semantics of transactions (see e.g., [GarM83]) or semantics of objects [Weih88],[BaRa92]. The utilization of transaction semantics is demonstrated in [GMol83] (also described in [CeGM88]), where transactions are classified into types and a compatibility set is associated with different types. A semantics based concurrency control method for objects is based on commutativity of operations. *Recoverability of operations* is an extension of this concept, which allows an invoked operation to proceed when it is recoverable with respect to an uncommitted operation [BaRa92]. Various operations on stacks and tables belong to this category. Two methods based on commutativity of operations are presented in [Weih88], which differ in that one method uses intention lists and the other uses undo logs. The formal approach appearing in this work is extended in [LMWF94]. Object-oriented DBMSs allow a higher degree of concurrency than provided by simple locking for operations on *abstract data types* [SkZd89],[Ozsu94]. A more detailed discussion of these topics appears in [RaCh96].

3.7 Locking in DB2

In order to put our discussion into a proper perspective, we give an overview of concurrency control in a mature relational DBMS, i.e., Version 4 for IBM's DB2 [IBMC95].

There are two types of objects in a DB2 database: tables and indexes. One or more tables may be held in a tablespace, which may be partitioned, simple, or segmented. Partitioning is applied when the tablespace holds a possibly single table which is very large. Each partition can be locked separately. In a simple (nonsegmented) tablespaces the entries of different tables might be interspersed in a page, while this is not so in a segmented tablespace. DB2's Version 4 has page as well as finer granularity row level locking.

The granularity of locking is specified using the LOCKSIZE clause at the time a tablespace is created. The various options are: TABLESPACE, TABLE, PAGE, ROW, and ANY. DB2 chooses the size of the lock with the ANY option, which is the default.

The issue of granularity of locking has been addressed in numerous earlier studies. An example from [IBMC95] on row versus page locking is used here to discuss the subtleties of this issue. Given 10 rows per page, It seems that locking the required row in the page, instead of the whole page, will reduce the level of lock contention by an order of magnitude. On the other hand, if two transactions are to lock in exclusive mode several rows in the page in different order, then the probability of deadlock has increased considerably. In case all the rows in a page are to be read, then we have increased the locking overhead by a factor of ten. However, DB2 can avoid acquiring a lock on data that has been committed using a technique called commit_LSN [Moha90], which is explained below.

Commit_LSN uses latches, which are an order of magnitude cheaper than locks, to assure that a page is not locked by figuring out that its contents are committed. This technique works in conjunction with the write ahead logging (WAL) protocol [GrRe92] and takes advantage of the log sequence number (LSN), which is a monotonically increasing function associated with log records written by WAL. Note that for recovery purposes each database page has a page_LSN, which is the LSN of the most recent update to the page. Let COMMIT_LSN refer to the LSN of the first log record of the *oldest* transaction in the system. If the page_LSN of a page to be accessed by a transaction is smaller than COMMIT_LSN it means that it is *not* being accessed by an active transaction and that its contents are committed.

The duration for which locks are held is determined by the *bind* option.[24] In static binding, where static SQL statements are bound before a program executes, the ACQUIRE and RELEASE options specify when DB2 locks a table or a tablespace and when it releases the lock. ACQUIRE(ALLOCATE) and ALLOCATE(USE) options acquire the lock when the program starts to run and when it first accesses it, respectively. RELEASE(DEALLOCATE) and RELEASE(COMMIT) release the lock when the application ends or commits, respectively.

The ACQUIRE(ALLOCATE) and RELEASE(DEALLOCATE) combination is similar to static locking, which provides efficient execution for batch applications. ACQUIRE(USE) and RELEASE(DEALLOCATE) combination is more efficient in that a table or tablespace is locked only if it is used while the

---

[24] The process of query compilation creates a control structure with access paths to data after authorization checking has been performed.

application is running. Unlike the previous combination deadlocks are a possibility. ACQUIRE(USE) and RELEASE(COMMIT) is the default combination.

Locks chosen by DB2 are obtained implicitly and depend on (i) the type of processing to be done; (ii) the value of LOCKSIZE for the target table; (iii) the *isolation* options (see discussion below). The exception is the overriding LOCK TABLE statement which may be in shared or exclusive mode and is intended for high priority applications.

ISOLATION options, which specify the extent at which read-only operations are isolated from the effect of other applications are as follows: RR (repeatable read), CS (cursor stability), and UR (uncommitted read) or write-through locks. With RR a row or page lock is held in shared or update mode till the next commit point, such that a row to be reread will not have changed since its previous reading. With CS a row or page lock is held long enough for the data to be read. The UR option is acceptable for applications willing to read modified but not necessarily committed data.

The ISOLATION(CS) option has the shortcoming that if a process reads a row and later returns to update it, then it may erase other updates to the row. One way around this problem is to use a cursor with the FOR UPDATE OF clause. Another way is to use the CURRENTDATA(YES) option, which effectively maintains a shared lock on the object being accessed.

Objects locked in DB2 are target tables and indexes, related tables to enforce referential integrity constraints [Date83],[GrRe92],[IBMC95] and DB2 internal objects, such as the DB2 catalog, etc. Two types of indexes are distinguished in the newest DB2 release: the older type I indexes are locked when the associated table, page, and rows are locked, while type II indexes are only locked if the value of the index is to be modified. However, all type II indexes on a table are protected by the corresponding locks on the table. The discussion in [Moha95] is applicable to type II index structures.

Intent locks provide a quick way to detect conflicts among transactions which intend to read or update a subset of the pages of a table or tablespace (the latter is not mentioned below for the sake of brevity).

- IS (intent share) mode locks on a table mean that the application can only read the contents of a table, after obtaining a page or row lock on the data to be read. Other transactions can read and update the contents of the table currently locked in IS mode.

- IX (intent exclusive) means that the lock owner and other applications can read and modify the contents of the table. The application should obtain appropriate locks on pages or rows it needs to update.

- SIX (share with intent exclusive) can read and change the data in a table, while other applications can only read its contents. A page or row level lock is required only for updates.

  Note that share (S), update (U), and exclusive (X) locks are also available at the level of tables or tablespaces. The following table is a compatibility matrix for table and tablespace locks.

Requested lock mode	Is the requested lock mode compatible with current lock mode (given below)?					
	IS	IX	S	U	SIX	X
IS	yes	yes	yes	yes	yes	no
IX	yes	yes	no	no	no	no
S	yes	no	yes	yes	no	no
U	yes	no	yes	no	no	no
SIX	yes	no	no	no	no	no
X	no	no	no	no	no	no

The reader is referred to [GrRe92] for further discussions of intent locks.

Lock promotion results in the exchange of a lock for a lock in a more restrictive mode. For page or row locks we have the promotion from S or U to X, while for table locks the promotion is from IS to IX or S and further to U, SIX, or X.

Lock escalation is intended for reducing locking overhead by escalating a large number or row or page level locks to a lock on a single table or tablespace. The LOCKMAX clause associated with creating or altering a table is the threshold beyond which lock escalation occurs.

Lock conflicts in DB2 are handled through a temporary *suspension* of the process requesting the lock. The process may timeout after its suspension period exceeds the timeout interval, which has a default value of 60 seconds. Deadlocks are resolved periodically and the default value for the period is 5 seconds.

The determination of the timeout interval for suspended transactions is somewhat complicated in DB2. This is best illustrated by a numerical example from [IBMC95]. Multiplying the rounded value of the ratio of RESOURCE TIMEOUT(=18) and DEADLOCK TIME(=5), i.e., ceil(18/5) = 4, by DEADLOCK TIME yields 20 sec. An application dependent TIMEOUT MULTIPLIER, which is greater than one, can be used to determine the timeout interval. Let us assume that its value for this type of processing is 3 and that the first scan occurs

4 seconds after the transaction is suspended. While it is noted that the process is suspended, this first occurrence is ignored. The suspended process is allowed to wait for 60 more seconds before it is timed out.

The EXPLAIN statement can be used to determine the locks chosen by DB2. This statement is used more generally to determine the access plan generated by the query optimizer to execute a query. More details appear in [IBMC95].

Statistical and accounting traces can be used to gather information about DB2 locking activities, which can then be summarized via the DB2 Performance Monitor (DB2 PM). These reports can be used to monitor the level of lock contention in the system.

Special locking modes are utilized by the utilities associated by DB2 which are beyond the scope of this discussion (see [IBMC95]).

CHAPTER 4: RESTART-ORIENTED LOCKING METHODS

Restart-oriented locking methods combine blocking and aborts (followed by restarts) to cope with the performance limits of standard locking. A subset of restart-oriented locking methods limit the wait depth of blocked transactions, where the wait depth is the distance of a blocked transaction from active transactions in the waits-for graph (it is shown below that this directed graph is acyclic). Wait depth limited methods are a subset of restart-oriented locking methods which limit d to a small value, $d = 0$ in the case of the no-waiting method and $d = 1$ in the case of some other methods discussed in this chapter. The *wait depth limited* **WDL** method [FrRT92] is a subset of wait depth limited methods, which in selecting the transaction to be aborted takes into account the progress made by conflicting transactions.

In the next section we first describe the restart-oriented locking methods, followed by options for restarting aborted transactions and the issue of re-sampling of lock requests. Section 4.3 provides a performance comparison of restart-oriented locking methods, based on simulation results reported in [Thom96]. The modeling of shared locks, in addition to exclusive locks, and hot-spots in the context of restart-oriented methods is described in Section 4.4. Finally, in Section 4.5 we review previous analytic studies of restart-oriented locking methods and provide the analysis of a representative method.

4.1 Description of Wait Depth Limited Locking Methods

A concise specification of some well-known restart-oriented locking methods is given below. Only exclusive locks are considered initially to simplify the discussion.

- According to the *no-waiting method* [TaSG85], also called the *immediate restart method* [AgCL87],[25] a transaction T_A which has a lock conflict with a transaction T_B is aborted. The waits-for graph $T_A \rightarrow T_B$ is temporarily formed and reduced.

- The *asymmetric running priority method* [FrRo85] aborts T_B in the waits-for graph $T_A \rightarrow T_B \rightarrow T_C$, when T_A becomes blocked by T_B, which is already blocked by T_C.[26] This action is expected to improve system performance, since it partially fulfills the *essential blocking property* that blocking is ac-

---

[25] We will not use this term, because it is used in Section 4.2 as an option for restarting aborted transactions.

[26] For the sake of brevity the waits-for graph does not depict all transactions, which are affected in a predictable manner, e.g., all blocked transactions activated by an abort. To clarify a perceived ambiguity in the specification of the asymmetric running priority method [HsZh92], consider another transaction T_D which was blocked by T_B while T_B was active. The lock request by T_A leads to $(T_A, T_D) \rightarrow T_B \rightarrow T_C$. Both T_D and T_A are activated when T_B is aborted, but in the case when both transactions have requested the same lock in an incompatible mode will result in T_D acquiring the lock and T_A remaining blocked by T_D, since locks are served in FCFS order.

ceptable only when the requested lock *is held by an active transaction do-ing useful work,* i.e., provided that the transaction will not be aborted at a later time [FrRo85].

It is possible that T_B, which was active at the time T_A became blocked by it, becomes blocked by T_C at a later time. When T_C is active, the *symmetric running priority* method [FrRT92] guarantees that the wait depth does not exceed one by aborting a transaction such as T_B, which is blocking other transactions when it encounters a lock conflict. Note that the essential blocking property is better satisfied by the symmetric running priority method than the asymmetric running priority method. Our implementation of the symmetric running priority method first checks whether a transaction T_A encountering a lock conflict is blocking other transactions and if so it is aborted; next it checks T_B by which T_A is blocked, and if T_B is blocked it is aborted. Simulation results have shown that changing the ordering of these two tests has little effect on overall performance.

An adaptive running priority method only aborts a transaction at $d = 1$ only if it is blocking $b \geq 1$ transactions, where b is referred to as transaction's breadth. The value of b can be varied to adjust the wasted processing based on processor utilization [FrRT91a] (see Section 5.4 in Chapter 5). Wasted processing can of course be reduced by increasing the wait depth $(d > 1)$. It is also meaningful to consider a combination of rules based on the wait depth and transaction's breadth, e.g., (i) if $d > 1$ and $b \geq 1$, (ii) if $d = 1$ and $b > 1$.

- The asymmetric cautious waiting method [HsZh92] aborts T_A when it is blocked by T_B which is itself blocked by T_C, as in $T_A \rightarrow T_B \rightarrow T_C$. The symmetric cautious waiting method first checks if T_A is blocking other transactions, as in $(T_X, T_Y, ..., T_Z) \rightarrow T_A \rightarrow T_B$, and aborts them when T_A becomes blocked.

Symmetric and asymmetric running priority and the cautious waiting methods are deadlock-free [FrRo85],[HsZh92].

- The WDL(d) method allows a wait depth d for blocked transaction [FrRT92]. The WDL(1) method, which is derived from the symmetric running priority method, is mainly of interest in high capacity systems [FrRT92]. Hence we use WDL to denote WDL(1). Conflicts are resolved by comparing the "length" of the transactions involved in the conflict. The length $L(T_A)$ of a transaction T_A is a function of the progress made by the transaction, e.g., the number of locks held by T_A [FrRT92]. The modified WDL method [Thom92b] is based on two slightly different rules from the WDL method [FrRT92], such that the lengths of only two transaction are compared at a time.

Consider a lock request by T_A which causes a lock conflict with T_B resulting in a *transient* waits-for graph $[(T_X, T_Y, ..., T_Z) \rightarrow]T_A \rightarrow T_B[\rightarrow T_C]$. The following rules are applied when a lock conflict occurs with the modified WDL method:

1. If T_A, which is blocking some other transactions, has a lock conflict with T_B, then if $L(T_A) < L(T_B)$ then abort T_A, else abort T_B.[27]

   The WDL method uses $L(T_A) < \max(L(T_B), L(T_X), ..., L(T_Z))$ when T_A is blocking transactions $(T_X, T_Y, ..., T_Z)$ [FrRT92].

2. If T_A, which is not blocking any other transactions, has a lock conflict with T_B, which is itself blocked by an active transaction (T_C), if $L(T_B) \leq L(T_C)$ then abort T_B, else abort T_C.

   The WDL method makes the comparison $L(T_B) \leq \max(L(T_A), L(T_C))$ [FrRT92].

It should be noted that the WDL family of methods allows a wait depth $d > 1$, but a wait depth of one yields the best performance when adequate hardware resources are available [FrRT92] (also see discussion in Section 4.3.2 of this paper and [Thom96]).

- The *wound-wait* method [RoSL78] blocks transaction T_A requesting a lock held by T_B if T_A is not older than T_B, otherwise T_B is aborted. Transaction age is determined by the timestamp of its arrival time.

- The *wait-die* method [RoSL78] allows a younger transaction to wait if it is blocked by an older transaction, otherwise the transaction encountering a lock conflict is aborted.

  Both the wound-wait and wait-die methods are deadlock-free [RoSL78], but allow unlimited wait depths. The wait-die method is not considered in this study, since according to simulation results reported in [ACMc87] the wound-wait method outperforms this method. This study also shows that the general waiting method is outperformed by the wound-wait method when intervening think times are allowed (see Section 2.1 in Chapter 2), which result in an increase in the degree of transaction concurrency and hence lock contention.

The no-waiting and cautious waiting methods and the method in [ChGM83] (see Section 4.5) are *nonpreemptive locking methods* [HsZh92], in that the transaction encountering a lock conflict is aborted, while according to this definition the running priority method is a *preemptive locking method*. Note that the state of transactions involved in a lock conflict affects cautious waiting, running priority, and the WDL and modified WDL methods. A classification is also possible based on transaction attributes used in determining the transaction to be aborted (if any). The wound-wait method and the wait-die meth-

---

[27] We could have used $L(T_A) > L(T_B)$ instead of $L(T_A) \geq L(T_B)$ for the else condition and a tie-breaking rule for equality, e.g., abort the younger transaction. This extra complication is not expected to result in an improvement in performance.

ods use a *static attribute,* i.e., transaction timestamps,[28] while the WDL method uses a *dynamic attribute,* since the number of locks held by a transaction varies with time.

4.2 Transaction Aborts and Restarts

Unlike some earlier works which use the terms "transaction abort" and "transaction restart" interchangeably, we distinguish between the two terms in this discussion. Transaction abort occurs first and a transaction stops execution and releases all of its locks. Aborted transactions are automatically restarted by the system. As described in Chapter 5, transaction aborts can be simulated by continuing to run a transaction in virtual execution mode [FrRT90],[FrRT92].

Cyclic restarts or *livelocks* are possible in conjunction with restart-oriented locking methods, including transaction aborts to resolve deadlocks, and are manifested by repeated conflicts among two or more transactions when they are restarted [ACMc87],[BeHG87],[GrRe92]. Cyclic restarts need to be prevented: (i) to reduce the wasted processing incurred in this manner; (ii) to ensure transaction completion within a finite time interval.[29] One of the following methods can be used for this purpose.

1. *Restart waiting* can be easily implemented in a centralized system by delaying the restart of an aborted transaction until *all* transactions which have conflicted with it are completed [RyTh90b],[FrRT92]. This has the advantage of reducing lock holding time, since a delayed transaction will be less susceptible to blocking when it is restarted.

2. *Random restart delays or conflict avoidance delays* [ACMc87], [AgCL87],[TayY87] do not guarantee that cyclic restarts will be prevented, especially in the case of variable size transactions. The main difficulty with using this method is the determination of the duration of the random delay. It is best to gradually increase the random delay with each successive restart incurred by a transaction, which is a method also used in multiple access communication protocols [Tasa86].

3. *Immediate restarts* are possible in a system with a backlog of transactions, such that an aborted transaction is set aside and is replaced by a new transaction with a different *script* [TaSG85],[AgCL87] (a transaction's script is defined as the sequence of objects accessed by it). Another interpretation is that the restarted transaction requests a different set of locks from its prior execution, i.e., the transaction does not exhibit *access invariance*

---

[28] Timestamps are not reassigned when the transaction is aborted in this case, i.e., timestamps are static across transaction executions, which is not the case for the timestamp ordering method (see Chapter 6).

[29] A program which simulates a concurrency control method involving cyclic restarts will not attain steady-state behavior and yield steady-state results [Lave83], since the number of transactions involved in cyclic restarts, which do not contribute to effective throughput is unpredictable. Simulation runs with different seeds for the random number generator will thus lead to different results.

[FrRT90],[FrRT92]. This is referred to as *lock resampling upon transaction restart* or a *fake restart,* as opposed to *no lock resampling upon transaction restart.* A performance study should take into account the delay encountered by aborted transactions which are set aside.

The restart waiting-no lock resampling option is mainly of interest in this paper, where the latter concurs with access invariance across successive executions of a restarted transaction.

An inherent shortcoming of the analytic solution methods is lock resampling, which results in overestimating system performance by an extent which depends on the frequency of transaction restarts. For example, simulation results with the random delay-no lock resampling option in Section 6.1 of [AgCL87] show that the immediate restart-lock resampling option in the case of the no-waiting method overestimates peak system throughput by as much as 30%. This effect is expected to be less significant when the random delay or restart waiting options are in effect, since by the time an aborted transaction is restarted, transactions conflicting with its script have left the system. In any case methods introducing frequent aborts and restarts benefit more from lock resampling than other methods with less frequent aborts.

An analytic solution for performance comparison poses difficulties as follows: (i) a fair comparison with the random delay option requires the tuning of the duration of the random delay, especially in the case of variable size transactions when transaction size is not known a priori. Tuning this delay would require extensive simulations, partially alleviating the advantage of an analytic solution; (ii) analytic solutions cannot predict the peak throughput of the modified WDL method accurately and hence an analysis of the WDL method was not even attempted [Thom92b]; (iii) the analysis to estimate the delay due to the restart waiting option, demonstrated in [RyTh90b] for the no-waiting method when there is only one transaction delaying the restart (in the case of exclusive lock requests), is expected to be much more complicated when multiple transactions are involved; (iv) analytic solutions for restart-oriented locking methods cannot be easily extended to handle exclusive and shared locks and hot-spots. Although the aforementioned difficulties with analytical modeling may not be unsurmountable, it was decided to use simulation with the restart waiting-no lock resampling option for the performance comparison, because restart waiting prevents cyclic restarts and the no lock resampling option provides a fair estimate of the relative performance of restart-oriented lock conflict resolution methods.

Resampling applies to locking modes (shared versus exclusive mode and whether an access is to a hot-spot or not) and the class of restarted transactions in a system with multiple transaction classes. The latter has been a problem area in some of the earlier analytic studies (see Section 4.5).

Resampling also applies to transaction processing times and results in an unfair advantage to methods with more frequent restarts, since this biases the completed transactions in the system towards transactions with shorter processing times, resulting in overestimating system performance. Of course transaction processing times may vary from one execution to the other as in the case of two-phase processing methods, but even in this case the execution time would be expected to remain the same following the first execution phase (see Chapter 5). The resampling of processing times can be prevented by generating them at the arrival time of a transaction and utilizing the same processing times for all transaction executions. This effect is especially significant in a system with optimistic concurrency control. As discussed in Section 5.5 in Chapter 5 special precautions are required in the analysis to ensure that transaction processing times are not resampled across executions.

4.3 Performance Comparison of Restart-Oriented Locking Methods

There have been several simulation studies involving restart-oriented locking methods, most notably [ACMc87],[FrRT92]. We summarize here the results of a simulation study with the restart waiting-no lock resampling option and exclusive lock requests to compare the performance of eight methods: the general waiting method, no-waiting method, symmetric cautious waiting method, symmetric running priority method, and the asymmetric running priority method, the WDL method, the modified WDL method, and the wound-wait method [Thom96]. The simulation parameters are as follows: database size $D = 16,384$, transaction size $K = 16$, and $K + 1$ exponentially distributed transaction steps with a mean processing time $s = 0.01$. The restart waiting-no lock resampling option is used in the simulation, which as explained in Section 4.2 is expected to provide a fair comparison. The number of transactions is varied to obtain the peak throughput for different hardware resource contention levels, which is attained by varying the number of processors in the system (P).

- The general waiting method outperforms other methods for smaller values of P, but achieves its maximum throughput at $\hat{M} \simeq 78$ with $\overline{M}_a = 55$ active transactions, i.e., the general waiting method can utilize at most $P = 55$ processors. Note also that there is little difference in the peak throughput attained by different methods at $P = 50$.

- The no-waiting method is outperformed by the general waiting method at $P = 50$, but the no-waiting method outperforms the general waiting method by almost 20% at $P = 100$ and its throughput continues to increase up to $P = 250$.

The no-waiting method with the immediate restart-lock resampling option is susceptible to thrashing due to repeated restarts. In fact a reduction in effective throughput beyond peak throughput can be observed as part of validation results in [TayY87]. The restart waiting-with no lock resampling option has the beneficial effect that the reduction in effective throughput beyond the peak point is gradual.

- The symmetric cautious waiting method introduces a significant improvement in performance with respect to the no-waiting method, which is due to the reduction in wasted processing. This is also the case for the asymmetric cautious waiting method [HsZh92]. Simulation results show that the symmetric and asymmetric cautious waiting methods have a comparable performance (differing by a few percentage points) and as would be expected the symmetric cautious waiting method outperforms (is outperformed by) the asymmetric cautious waiting method for small (respectively large) values of P, since the asymmetric cautious waiting method introduces fewer aborts than the symmetric cautious waiting method.

- The symmetric running priority method outperforms symmetric cautious waiting method in all cases, which is attributable to the fact that aborting a blocked transaction in the case of the symmetric running priority method results in an increase in the number of active transactions from one active transaction in $T_A \rightarrow T_B \rightarrow T_C$ to two active transactions (T_A and T_C) when T_B is aborted and starts restart waiting, while with the symmetric cautious waiting method an aborted transaction just starts restart waiting, since an immediate restart will lead to repeated conflicts and aborts [HsZh92].

  It is interesting to note that for smaller values of P the asymmetric running priority method not only outperforms the symmetric running priority method, but also the WDL and modified WDL methods, which is attributable to the fact that the asymmetric running priority method results in less wasted processing than the other methods, such that it can maximize the useful processing in the system.

- The original WDL [FrRT92] and the modified WDL [Thom92b] methods outperform others (including the asymmetric running priority method) at higher processing capacities. The peak throughput attained by these two methods is almost a factor of four higher than that attained by the general waiting method and 20% higher than the asymmetric running priority method. These results concur with earlier simulation results [FrRT92]. It is interesting to note that the modified WDL method, in spite of its relative simplicity with respect to the original WDL method, attains a performance very close to it.

- The wound-wait method, while outperforming the general waiting method for higher values of P, is outperformed by all other methods, except the no-waiting method. The fact that transactions are blocked in timestamp order results in a very little drop in peak throughput once it is attained. In effect unnecessary restarts are avoided and the restart waiting option is not required in this case. This behavior is also observed in [FHRT93].

A simulation study using a synthetic workload and a lock trace are used in [WHMZ94] to compare the performance of several load control methods, especially those based on conflict ratios (see Section 3.2 in Chapter 3). The WDL method is shown to have a superior performance in all cases, but one, which is an accelerated synthetic workload. The reason for this is WDL's smaller lock waiting time with respect to other methods. Note that unlike some of the other methods considered, the WDL method per se does not have an explicit admission control method, i.e., transactions arriving at the system are activated immediately, but restart waiting serves as a load control mechanism.

The method with the maximum effective throughput for a given P maximizes the number of processors doing useful work (say P_u). Thus for intermediate values of P considered in [Thom96] the asymmetric running priority method outperforms the WDL method since it attains a higher P_u. However, as P is increased, the WDL method is able to utilize more processors and attains a higher P_u than the asymmetric running priority method. In fact for the simulation parameters resulting in the lock contention level introduced per transaction, even the WDL method and the modified WDL method cannot utilize more than $P = 500$ processors.

Synthesizing the method maximizing system throughput remains an open problem. Some guidelines for this purpose are as follows:

1. From the viewpoint of data contention it should conform with the essential blocking property [FrRo85] and minimize wasted lock holding time, which may affect system performance when lock utilizations are high, e.g., locks on hot-spots.[30]

2. From the viewpoint of hardware resource contention it should minimize wasted processing by associating a higher priority with transactions which have attained more processing [FrRT92] and exhibit adaptiveness to system load, e.g., by reducing the number of transaction aborts when the system is overloaded [FrRT91a]. As discussed in Section 5.4 in Chapter 5 the effective throughput is maximized when the bottleneck resource in the system is highly (but not fully) utilized. This ensures that the wasted processing in the system is minimized and the useful processing is maximized.

Generally there may be a tradeoff balancing wasted lock utilization and wasted hardware processing in selecting transactions to abort, but this is not usually the case, because the processing acquired by a transaction

---

[30] Consider a hypothetical system where a single frequently accessed lock constitutes the system bottleneck, while other locks are accessed infrequently. The system throughput can be maximized by minimizing the wasted utilization of this lock. Lock holding time is wasted if a transaction holding the lock is aborted or if it is blocked by another transaction, i.e., it does not progress at full speed. Thus the transaction scheduler for this idealized system should abort all transactions which get in the way of the transaction holding the hot-spot lock.

tends to be highly correlated with the number of locks that it holds. In fact these two parameters tend to be proportional to each other in most simulation studies. Further investigations are required to determine how to balance the wasted processing versus wasted lock holding time in systems where the number of locks held by transactions is not correlated with the processing acquired by them. Minimizing wasted lock holding time is more important in cases when there are a few hot-spots governing the maximum throughput, while minimizing wasted CPU processing is important when the CPU is near saturation.

3. Transaction response times can be reduced by not aborting transactions near their completion, although they may have not entered the commit state yet. This information can be deduced quite accurately from the transaction type in some cases. A by-product of this guideline is of course the reduction in lock holding time and transaction processing time.

Given that the future lock requests are known a priori, an "optimal" method can be used to determine the best possible performance, e.g., the minimum mean response time for a given throughput, against which other methods can be gauged. Unfortunately, optimal policies for this purpose are expected to be computationally very expensive. In contrast, once the trace of page requests is known, the optimal method for minimizing the miss ratio in paging virtual memory systems is to simply replace the page referenced furthest in the future [CoDe73].

The performance of methods based on optimistic concurrency control and access invariance is compared to restart-oriented locking methods in Section 5.4 in Chapter 5.

4.4 Modeling the Effect of Shared Locks and Hot-Spots on Performance

It is important to determine if the relative performance of the restart-oriented locking methods in the presence of shared as well as exclusive locks and hot-spots and whether the effective database size paradigm [TayY87], defined in Section 3.4 in Chapter 3 is also applicable to restart-oriented locking methods.

To answer the first question we extend the specification of the asymmetric running priority method to handle shared locks, while preventing deadlocks: restart all transactions holding the requested lock in shared mode if only one of them is to be aborted, because it is blocked. Simulation results in a system with infinite resources show that this method outperforms the general waiting method [Thom96], which may not be true in a system with limited hardware resources.

The effective database size paradigm is expected to be applicable to the restart-oriented locking methods, since they simply maintain a subset of the waits-for graph of the general waiting method, but this is not always so. For example, according to Corollary 5.2 in [TaSG85], the effective database size paradigm for shared and exclusive locks for the no-waiting method with the lock resampling option holds only *for sufficiently low levels of lock contention.* This problem is considered in detail in [HsZh95] in the context of the no-waiting method and asymmetric cautious waiting method, which are "equal chance abort policies", i.e., the probability of transaction abort upon a lock request is independent of its current state. The data flow balance principle is used in the context of the hot-spot database access model to show that the effective database size (D_{eff}) is an increasing function of M and that the effective database size paradigm underestimates D_{eff} by estimating it at $M = 0$. The effective database size paradigm overestimates the lock conflict probability, since it does not take into account the lock resampling effect. This analysis in [HsZh95] is of limited applicability, since it deals with the less realistic lock resampling option (see discussion of access invariance in Section 5.1).

It follows from simulation results in [Thom96] that the effective database size paradigm provides an acceptably accurate approximation for the no lock resampling option (this includes no resampling of locking modes). For this purpose we consider the no-waiting method, which introduces the most aborts among the restart-oriented locking methods discussed in this study. Simulation results show that performance metrics obtained by applying the effective database size paradigm to shared and exclusive locks are indistinguishable from the results for the original model and that very close results are obtained with the hot-spot model. Based on these experiments it is conjectured that the effective database size paradigm applies approximately to the no-waiting and asymmetric cautious waiting methods for which the transaction making the lock request is aborted. This is attributed to the fact that the expected mix of the modes of locks held by transactions in the system is only affected by the last lock request of an aborted transaction. However, there is the second order effect that a transaction making an exclusive lock request has a higher probability of lock conflict than when it makes a shared lock request.

In the case of the asymmetric running priority method it is observed from simulation results that the throughput obtained by applying the effective database size paradigm to the hot-spot model matches the throughput obtained by the original model quite well. The peak system throughput is typically overestimated by 5%. The reason that the two systems are not equivalent is that the length function used by the modified WDL method is based on the number of locks held by a transaction in different regions. The performance of the system can be improved by assigning a higher weight to hot-spots. The length function of a transaction can be specified as a weighted sum of the number of locks held in different database regions. The weighing factors b^2/c and $(1 - b)^2/(1 - c)$ may be appropriate for the number of hot-spots and cold-spots, respectively. The choice of appropriate weighing factors and their effect on improving system performance remains an area of further investigation.

The effective database size paradigm is less accurate in the case of the asymmetric running priority method when applied to a system with shared and exclusive locks. This is attributable to the fact that the composition of transactions in the system is affected when transactions are aborted as a result of a lock conflict (as in the case of multiple transactions holding a lock in shared mode being aborted because one of them is blocked).

Restarts with resampling of locking modes have a tendency of decreasing the level of lock contention in the system, since transactions introducing less lock contention have a higher probability of committing successfully. This problem can be fixed in a simulation study by maintaining the same locks and locking modes (shared or exclusive) across executions. A technique to alleviate the resampling of locking modes in analytical modeling is discussed in the next section.

4.5 Performance Analyses of Restart-Oriented Locking Methods

We briefly review earlier analytic studies of the restart-oriented locking methods. We next illustrate the analysis of a nontrivial wait depth limited method by analyzing the performance of the symmetric running priority method.

4.5.1 Review of Earlier Analytic Studies

The first paper dealing with the analysis of the no-waiting method as a means to obtain a worst case bound for the general waiting method is [ShSp81] (that the no-waiting method is not always outperformed by the general waiting method was shown in [TaGS85], also see [RyTh90b]). A method according to which a transaction encountering a lock conflict repeats its request L times before it is aborted is described in [ChGM83]. A Markov chain model representing the progress of a single transaction is used to analyze system performance. Numerical results with lock resampling-immediate restart option and infinite resource assumptions lead to the conclusion that the best performance is attained at $L = 0$, i.e., the no-waiting method. Comprehensive studies of the no-waiting method and the general waiting method using flow diagrams appear in [TaSG85] and [TaGS85], respectively (see also [TayY87]). It is shown in [TaGS85] that the no-waiting method outperforms the general waiting method when there are infinite resources, but at lower degrees of transaction concurrency the no-waiting method is outperformed by the general waiting method (by at most 5%). Another study [RyTh90b] concludes that the general waiting method outperforms the no-waiting method in its nonthrashing region, unless there are infinite resources and the immediate restart-lock resampling option is in effect. The flow diagram method of [TayY87] is adopted to the analysis of the asymmetric cautious waiting method in [HsZh92].

4.5.2 Flow Diagram, Semi-Markov Chain, and Markov Chain Models

The analysis in this case is simplified by considering the execution of one transaction as affected by the remaining transactions in the system from the hardware and data resource contention viewpoint. The flow diagram or semi-Markov chain [Klei75] depicting the execution steps of a transaction T of size K is shown in Figure 3.1. S_{2i}, $0 \leq i \leq K$ (respectively S_{2i+1}, $0 \leq i \leq K - 1$) correspond to active (respectively blocked) states. The transition rates among the states are derived below, but it should be noted that the transition $S_{2K} \rightarrow S_0$ stands for the completion of a transaction and its immediate replacement by another transaction, according to the closed system paradigm.

Semi-Markov chains allow a general distribution for state holding time, while Markov chains stipulate an exponential distribution [Klei75]. The use of semi-Markov chains in the analysis of the general waiting, the no-waiting, and the asymmetric cautious waiting policies in [TaGS85],[TaSG85],[HsZh92], respectively is possible because all transitions from the active state occur at the time the transaction completes its processing and makes a lock request and that only one transition is possible from the blocked state. The symmetric running priority method, the asymmetric running priority method, and the WDL methods abort a transaction in the blocked state, i.e., there are two transitions from this state, which requires determining the distribution of waiting time. This is expensive computationally as explained in Section 4.5.6 and in [Thom95b]. We therefore assume that waiting times are exponentially distributed. The additional assumption that the transaction abort process is Poisson, which is similar to the one used in analyzing the optimistic concurrency control method in Section 5.5 in Chapter 5, leads to a low cost solution for the semi-Markov chain model. Since the distribution of transaction steps has little effect on performance and to simplify the analysis one step further, we assume that the processing times of transaction steps are exponentially distributed, such that a Markov chain analysis is possible.

The state equilibrium equations for the Markov chain can be solved easily to obtain the steady-state probabilities π_i, $0 \leq i \leq 2K$ [Klei75]. The mean number of visits to S_i (v_i) can be similarly obtained by noting that $v_{2K} = 1$. Given that h_i denotes the mean holding time at S_i then $\pi_i = v_i h_i / \sum_{j=0}^{2K} v_j h_j$, $0 \leq i \leq 2K$.

Note that $v_0 - 1$ denotes the mean number of transaction aborts.

Random delays preceding transaction restart can be incorporated into the analysis by introducing an extra state preceding the initial state when a transaction is aborted (refer to Figures 10 and 25 in [TaSG85] and [TayY87], respectively). The overhead of aborting a transaction, e.g., the undoing of transaction updates [BeHG87],[GrRe92], can be taken into account by intro-

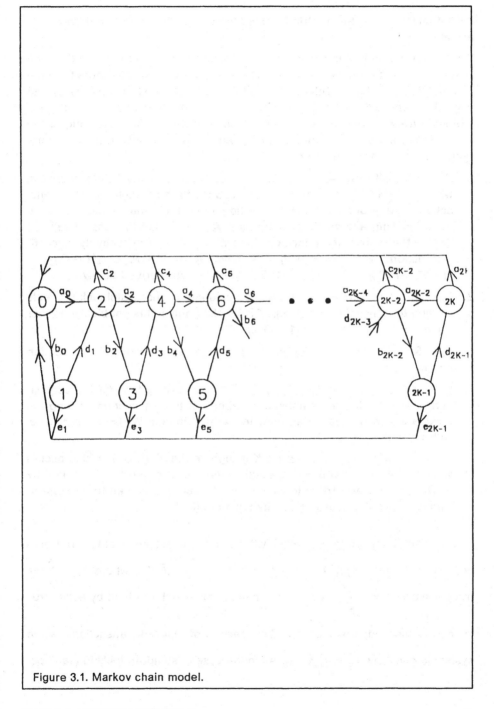

Figure 3.1. Markov chain model.

ducing additional "secondary" states corresponding to the "primary" states in the Markov chain (see e.g., Figure 22 in [TayY87]).

4.5.3 Analysis of the Symmetric Running Priority Method with Fixed Transaction Sizes

This analysis is intended to illustrate a general solution method based on the progress made by transactions, as in [TaSG85],[TayY87], which differs from the Markov chain model in [ThRy83],[RyTh88] (see Section 3.3 in Chapter 3) and [RyTh90a], where the state is determined by the number of active transactions. The state transition rates of the Markov chain in Figure 3.1 according to the symmetric running priority method are given below. The unknown parameters required for this analysis are derived later.

1. $S_{2j} \rightarrow S_{2j+2}$ with rate a_{2j}, $0 \leq j \leq K - 1$ designate successful lock requests, while $S_{2K} \rightarrow S_0$ with rate $a_{2K} = \mu_K$ corresponds to the completion of a transaction. The probability that transaction T encountering a lock conflict at S_{2j} is blocking another transaction is given by Q_j. Let P_a (respectively P_b) denote the probability of lock conflict with an active (respectively blocked) transaction, with $P_c = P_a + P_b$. We have $a_{2j} = [(1 - P_c) + P_b(1 - Q_j)]\mu_j = (1 - P_a - P_bQ_j)\mu_j$, $0 \leq j \leq K - 1$. P_a, P_b, and Q_j are derived below.

2. $S_{2j} \rightarrow S_{2j+1}$ with rate b_{2j}, $1 \leq j \leq K - 1$ designate unsuccessful lock requests leading to transaction blocking. T is blocked only if it is not blocking other transactions, hence $b_{2j} = P_a(1 - Q_j)\mu_j$, $0 \leq j \leq K - 1$.

3. $S_{2j} \rightarrow S_0$ with rate $c_{2j} = P_cQ_j\mu_j$, $1 \leq j \leq K - 1$ correspond to transaction aborts.

4. $S_{2j+1} \rightarrow S_{2j+2}$ with rate d_{2j+1}, $0 \leq j \leq K - 1$. The waiting time for the acquisition of a lock (due to completion or abort of the transaction holding the lock) is approximated by an exponential distribution $W(t) = 1 - e^{-\nu t}, t \geq 0$, with $\nu = 1/W$.

5. $S_{2j+1} \rightarrow S_0$ with rate e_{2j+1}, $0 \leq j \leq K$ designate the abort of T, which occurs when T', which is not blocking other transactions, requests a lock held by T. The process according to which T is aborted is assumed to be Poisson with rate ω_j at S_{2j+1}. ω_j is given by equation (3.4).

The probability of lock conflict with active (respectively blocked) transactions is $P_a \approx (M - 1)\bar{L}_a/D$ (respectively $P_b \approx (M - 1)\bar{L}_b/D$), where $\bar{L}_a = \sum_{j=1}^{K} j\pi_{2j}$ (respectively $\bar{L}_b = \sum_{j=1}^{K-1} j \pi_{2j+1}$) is the mean number of locks held by active (respectively blocked) transactions. The fraction of blocked transactions in the system is given by $\beta (= \sum_{j=1}^{K} \pi_{2j-1})$. As in the case of standard locking (see Section 3.1 in Chapter 3) the mean number of active and blocked transactions is $\overline{M}_a = M(1 - \beta)$ and $\overline{M}_b = M\beta$, respectively. The mean number of locks held per transaction is $\overline{L} = \overline{L}_a + \overline{L}_b$ and hence $P_c \simeq (M - 1)\overline{L}/D$. The probability that T at S_{2j} is blocking at least one of the $\overline{M}_b$ blocked transactions in the system is approximated by

$$Q_j = 1 - [1 - j/(M\overline{L}_a)]^{\overline{M}_b}, \quad 1 \le j \le K, \tag{4.1}$$

$j/(M\overline{L}_a)$ is the probability that another transaction is blocked by the target transaction at S_{2j} (the denominator denotes the mean number of locks held by active transactions).

The mean waiting time W_j due to a lock conflict with an active transaction at S_{2j} is $W_j = \sum_{l \ge 2j}^{2K} v'_l h_l$. The mean holding time in S_l is $h_l = s_i = 1/\mu_i$ when $l = 2i$, $j \le i \le K$. The mean residual processing time at S_{2j} equals the processing time in that step, since the per step processing times are exponentially distributed [Klei75]. The mean waiting time in the blocked state S_l is the expected value of the minimum of two exponential distributions $h_l = 1/(\omega_i + v)$ with $l = 2i + 1$, $j \le i \le K - 1$. The primed visit ratios are introduced to take into account the fact that the state of the blocking transaction at which the lock conflict occurs is visited once by the blocked transaction and we need to compute the mean number of visits with respect to this state. The visit ratios for the current execution instance with respect to S_{2j} are computed by setting $v'_{2j} = 1$, and recursively computing the probabilities of visiting successive active and blocked states, i.e., $v'_{2i+1} = b_{2i}v'_{2i}$ and $v'_{2i+2} = (a_{2i} + b_{2i}d_{2i+1})v'_{2i}$, $j \le i \le K$, which takes into account the fact that a transaction may obtain its locks due to a transaction completion or abort. The mean waiting time is given by

$$W = \sum_{j=1}^{K} q_j W_j, \tag{4.2}$$

where q_j is the probability of lock conflict with an active transaction at S_{2j}. The probability q_j equals the time-space product of the number of locks held at S_{2j} and their holding time: $q_j = j\pi_{2j}/H$, where $H = \sum_{j=1}^{K} j\pi_{2j}$ is a normalization constant.

The rate of lock requests by the other transactions in the system is

$$\lambda = (1 - \frac{1}{M})T(M) \sum_{l=0}^{K-1} v_{2l}(1 - Q_l). \tag{4.3}$$

The summation takes into account the increase in the rate of requested locks due to transaction restarts and the fact that lock conflicts due to transactions which are blocking other transactions do not have an effect, since these transactions are aborted upon lock conflict.

The analysis of the asymmetric running priority method can be accomplished by introducing additional levels of blocking, while the current analysis only allows one level of blocking. The level of blocking in the case of the asymmetric running priority method increases if the active transaction at the forefront of a chain of blocked transaction is blocked and decreases when it is completed. The mean blocking time in this case can be determined using the techniques which have appeared in [TaGS85],[HsZh92],[Thom93b].

The rate at which a transaction at S_{2j+1} is aborted is proportional to the number of locks that it holds

$$\omega_j = j\lambda/D, \quad 0 \leq j \leq K - 1. \tag{4.4}$$

The mean transaction response time is $R(M) = \sum_{j=0}^{K} v_{2j}s_j + \sum_{j=0}^{K-1} v_{2j+1}/(v + \omega_j)$.

Transaction throughput is given by $T(M) = M/R(M)$ or alternatively by $T(M) = M\mu_K\pi_{2K}$. Some of the parameters required for the analysis are not known a priori, hence an iterative solution is required, which tends to converge in a few cycles.

Validation with the infinite resources assumption shows the analysis of the symmetric running priority method to be quite accurate up to very high lock contention levels, but underestimates peak throughput by 8%, which is partially attributable to the fact that our analysis does not take into account the possibility of multiple transactions being unblocked when another transaction is aborted (this is verified by the simulation results in [Thom95b]).

In the case of the no-waiting method, there are only two transition types: $a_{2j} = \mu_j(1 - P_a)$, $0 \leq j \leq K - 1$ and $c_{2j-1} = \mu_j P_a$, $0 \leq j \leq K$. It can be easily shown that $\pi_{2j} = \pi_0(1 - P_a)^j$, $1 \leq j \leq K$. Multiplying both sides of this equation by M yields the mean number of transactions in different states, as obtained by the analysis of flow diagrams in [TaSG85],[TayY87]. It is shown in [TaSG85], [TayY87] that the analysis in this case is tantamount to solving a polynomial equation in $q \triangleq 1 - P_a$, which is derivable from the last equation noting that

$P_a \simeq \overline{N}/D$, where $\overline{N} = M \sum_{j=1}^{K} j \pi_j$ is the mean number of locks held in the system

(using M instead of $M - 1$ in other studies makes little difference at higher degrees of concurrency). It is shown in [TaSG85],[TayY87] that the polynomial has a unique root in the range (0,1).

In the case of the general waiting method there are three transition types, provided that as in [TaGS85] we ignore the effect of deadlocks: $a_{2j} = \mu_j(1 - P_c)$, $0 \le j \le K - 1$ and $b_{2j} = \mu_j P_c$, $0 \le j \le K$, and $d_{2j-1} = v = 1/W$, $1 \le j \le K$. The state equilibrium equations are given by $\pi_{2j-1} = (\mu P_c/v)\pi_{2j-2}$, $1 \le j \le K$ and $\pi_{2j} = \pi_0 = [1 + K(1 + \mu P_c/v)]^{-1}$, $1 \le j \le K$. That active states and blocked states have equal probabilities was stated in Section 3.4 in Chapter 3, based on an intuitive argument. System performance in this case depends on P_c and $v = 1/W$. Multiple levels of transaction blocking need to be considered in estimating W in this case [TaGS85],[ThRy91],[Thom93b].

4.5.4 Analysis of the Symmetric Running Priority Method with Variable Transaction Sizes

The analysis of a frequency based model of the no-waiting method in [TaSG85], (Section 2.5 in [TayY87]) uses different transition points from a single flow diagram to denote transaction completions. This analysis does not assure *conservation of transaction frequencies*, i.e., the fraction of transactions completed by the system differs from the original frequencies in a manner favoring shorter transactions, which have a higher probability of success than longer transactions (this statement follows from the above analysis of the no-waiting method). In Section 2.3 of [TayY87] and [TaSG85] a system with a given number of transactions in two classes is analyzed by a simple extension of the analysis for a single class. The original transaction frequencies in a system with multiple classes can be maintained by utilizing a separate Markov chain per transaction class [Thom92b],[Thom95b].

4.5.5 Resampling of Locking Modes in Analytic Studies

The problem of resampling of locking modes can be resolved in the same manner as that of resampling of transaction sizes, i.e., by considering an appropriate number of transaction classes. Let us consider the case of modeling shared and exclusive locks for transactions with fixed size K (the fraction of exclusive locks is denoted by f_x as before). Taking into account all possible sequences of shared and exclusive lock requests requires 2^K transaction classes, which is not feasible computationally. Only $K + 1$ transaction classes with frequencies $\binom{K}{n} f_x^n (1 - f_x)^{K-n}$, $0 \le n \le K$ are required to fix the average number of exclusive lock requests. This does not however yield the same mean for the number of exclusive locks held per transaction, since the steps at which exclusive locks are requested are resampled. *Read-write-phased* transactions [HsZh92], as in [AgCL87], where all shared lock requests precede exclusive lock requests, are expected to minimize the lock contention level, since the mean number of exclusive locks held per transaction is the smallest in this case. Finally, a single transaction class with $(1 - f_x)K$ shared locks preceding the $f_x K$ exclusive locks can be postulated to obtain an upper bound to system performance[31] (a lower bound is similarly obtained by requesting the exclusive locks first). This discussion illustrates the sensitivity of system performance to the underlying database access model as far as locking modes are concerned. In its current form the effective database size paradigm is only applicable to database access models, where the lock request mode is determined by a Bernoulli trial. To estimate the lock conflict probability otherwise we need to take into account the holding times of shared and exclusive locks based on the step at which they are requested.

4.5.6 More on Semi-Markov Chain Models

The solution of the semi-Markov chain model requires the mean number of visits to each state (v_i) which can be directly obtained from the state equilibrium equations corresponding to Figure 3.1 by substituting the state transition rates with state transition probabilities (indicated by primes) and replacing π's with v's and noting that $v_{2K} = 1$, since S_{2K} is entered once signifying transaction completion. The transition probability associated with a link exiting a node is the ratio of the transition rate on the link and the sum of transition rates from that node, i.e., $a'_j = a_j/\mu_j$, $b'_j = b_j/\mu_j$, $c'_j = c_j/\mu_j$. Also $d'_{2j+1} = v/(v + \omega_j)$ and $e'_{2j+1} = \omega_j/(v + \omega_j)$.

In the case of a semi-Markov chain the transition probabilities can be determined as follows. Given that the time to release a lock has a distribution $W(t)$ and the rate at which a blocked transaction is aborted is ω_j then $e'_j = P_j^{Abort} = \int_0^\infty P_j(t)dW_j(t)$, where $P_j(t) = 1 - e^{-\omega_j t}$. $W_j(t)$ is a weighted sum of the distributions of delays, which can be expressed as the sums of random variables associated with the states leading to transaction commit or abort. $W(0) = 1$ is an appropriate initialization. The solution method outlined above is quite expensive, since the iteration step requires numerical convolutions to obtain the probability distributions along different paths.

One approach to bypass this problem is to find an appropriate probability distribution to which the waiting time can be fitted. The (negative) exponential distribution is determined to be a good fit in [HsZh92], which has the advantage of requiring a single parameter. This leads to a simple solution even for semi-Markov chain models.

---

[31] When $(1 - f_x)K$ is not an integer we can take the ceiling and floor values in each case to obtain an upper and a lower bound in this case).

CHAPTER 5: TWO-PHASE PROCESSING METHODS

Optimistic concurrency control is a major alternative to locking [KuRo81], but is less suitable than locking in meeting the requirements of DBMSs for high performance transaction processing [Haer84],[Moha92b]. However, there have been many prototyping efforts [Robi82], [KeTe84], [LeRo85], [MuTa85], [Room82], numerous proposals for improved algorithms [MeNa82], [Robi84], [Haer84], [PrSU86], [BCFP87], [FrRT92], and several analyses of optimistic concurrency control performance [MeNa82],[MoWo85],[RyTh87]. Optimistic concurrency control has also been applied to operations on abstract data types [Herl90].

Section 5.1 is an introduction to optimistic concurrency control, which defines its three execution phases and contrasts it with locking. Section 5.2 describes several options for validating transactions in optimistic concurrency control. Mechanisms for transaction execution are described in Section 5.3. Two-phase processing methods using these mechanisms and a brief discussion of their relative performance with respect to each other and locking methods appears in Section 5.4. In Section 5.5 we outline analytic solution methods for optimistic concurrency control.

5.1 Introduction to Optimistic Concurrency Control

Standard locking and optimistic concurrency control are two extreme concurrency control methods, which ensure serializability through transaction blocking (aborts to resolve deadlocks are infrequent) and restarts, respectively. When the level of data contention is high standard locking tends to under-utilize hardware resources, because a significant fraction of activated transactions in the system may become blocked, while optimistic concurrency control results in wasted processing. This tradeoff has been quantified in numerous performance studies [MeNa82],[MoWo85],[AgCL87],[FrRo85], [FrRT92] and is discussed in Section 5.5.

The execution of a transaction with optimistic concurrency control comprises three phases [KuRo81]:

1. **Read phase.** This phase corresponds to standard transaction execution, during which a transaction accesses database objects and possibly updates them. A "clean" or committed copy of requested objects is made available to transactions from the (global) database buffer in this phase, while dirty copies of the same objects may exist in the *private workspace* of other transactions. Reciprocally, the updates (pre-writes) of transactions during the "read" phase do not affect the database buffer, but only transaction's private workspace.

2. **Validation phase.** This phase is required to ensure serializability by checking for data conflicts among transactions, as described in more detail in Section 5.2. Data conflicts are resolved by aborting transactions which fail their validation.

3. **Write phase.** After a successful validation a transaction which reads but does not update database objects is considered completed (some post-processing may be required depending on the implementation method as described in Section 5.2). A transaction which reads and updates database objects after a successful validation initiates commit processing (writing out of redo log records onto stable storage), externalizes or propagates modified data objects to the database buffer (note that no disk writes are required if a No-Force commit method is in effect [BeHG87], [GrRe92]), and carries out some post-processing.

A more detailed description of the validation phase appears in Section 5.2.

Both optimistic concurrency control and two-phase locking are inefficient when transactions update database hot-spots. Locking has been extended with *field calls* in IMS FastPath [GrRe92] to deal with the case when the hot-spot is an aggregate variable. The similarity between optimistic concurrency control and field calls method is considered in [GrRe92], which is repeated here in the context of an inventory control example based on an application adopted from [ONei87]. A transaction first tests that enough items are available (e.g. *QOH* $\geq$ *Request_size)* to satisfy a certain order and again before transaction commit. If the first (respectively second) test fails then the transaction follows an alternate path (respectively is aborted). What makes this method similar to optimistic concurrency control is that the object is not updated after the first test, but only after the second test is successful. Only one out of *M* transactions accessing and updating the *QOH* succeeds with optimistic concurrency control, while all *M* transactions will succeed with the field calls approach, as long as the *current* value of *QOH*, whose value may have been modified since it was first tested, exceeds *Request_size*. It should be noted that the field calls approach requires extra effort by the programmer, while the optimistic concurrency control method does not.

The following advantages are associated with optimistic concurrency control:

1. Performance evaluation studies have shown that optimistic concurrency control outperforms standard locking in high data contention systems, provided there are adequate hardware resources [FrRo85], [ThRy86], [AgCL87],[FrRT90],[FrRT92], although it may be argued that this is only so for unrealistically high lock contention levels.

2. While the first execution of a transaction in optimistic mode may be unsuccessful, it has the beneficial effect of "priming the buffer" for its re-

execution, which will tend to be very short since no disk I/O (or remote access) is required [MaNa82],[Robi84],[FrRT90],[FrRT92]. This is so provided *access invariance* prevails, i.e., that the set of objects accessed by a transaction is time-independent. Access invariance may be at a logical or a physical level, where the former (respectively latter) implies that a restarted transaction accesses the same set of objects (respectively objects residing on the same disk block) [FrRT90],[FrRT92]. Access invariance can be justified by the fact that although the state of a database varies with time (at a rate proportional to the throughput of transactions updating it), it does not vary fast enough to change the execution sequence or even the outcome of execution of a transaction when it is restarted. This is perhaps another reason why serializability is a sufficient correctness criterion. In the case of an airline reservation system, for example, while some tickets may have been sold on a popular flight since the time of a transaction's first execution, a sellout is not expected over a short period of time. A more comprehensive discussion of access invariance appears in [FrRT90],[FrRT92].

3. Locking in distributed, client-server, and data sharing environments (see Chapter 6) requires extra messages to request locks, even when the data is available locally (unless the data is protected by system locks as in data sharing systems described in Chapter 6 [Rahm93b]). When the data is cached locally, no inter-node communication is required with optimistic concurrency control, until the time of transaction validation [ThRa90], [Thom92a].

We also describe a set of transaction scheduling methods, which similarly to the optimistic die option (described in Section 5.2) take advantage of access invariance, but are based on locking, i.e., they may or may not use optimistic concurrency control's private workspace paradigm. Since aborts and restarts occur frequently with this method, it is important to ensure that transaction rollback can be carried out efficiently, e.g., log records to undo the updates of uncommitted transactions are kept in main storage [FrRT92].

5.2 Transaction Validation with Optimistic Concurrency Control

Three conditions for serialized execution of two transactions are [KuRo81]:

1. T_1 completes its write phase, before T_2 starts its read phase.

2. The write phase of T_1 and the read phase of T_2 overlap in time, but the writeset of T_1 does not overlap the readset of T_2.

3. The writeset of T_1 does not conflict with the readset or writeset of T_2 and T_1 completes its read phase before T_2 completes its read phase.

This validation method has the shortcoming of unnecessarily aborting transactions. This problem is fixed in [Robi84]. For example, the overlap of the access sets of T_1 and T_2 implies that T_2 has been conflicted by T_1. However, there is no data conflict if T_2 read an object written after T_1's commit [PrSU86]. Two validation methods for optimistic concurrency control, which alleviate false aborts, are described later in this section.

Two other problems associated with optimistic concurrency control according to [PrSU86] are: (i) the high risk of abort for long transactions; (ii) starvation due to permanent aborts, which is another form of livelock. The former problem can be resolved through versioning for transactions which only read the database. Approaches to deal with the second problem appear in Section 5.3. A method based on *substitute transactions* is described in [PrSU86], where this transaction is provided with the access-set of a transaction which has been aborted repeatedly. The substitute transaction has the role of making sure that no conflicting transaction (a transaction updating its access set) will commit successfully, while the original transaction is in progress. This method, similarly to those described in Section 5.4, is applicable when transactions exhibit access invariance and is effectively the same as preclaiming locks on relevant objects.

The implementation described in [MeNa82],[RyTh87] requires the association of a timestamp $t(O)$ with "active" database objects, which indicates the time at which object O was last updated. No timestamp is required for objects which are not currently being referenced and are possibly stored on disk. The following two rules are required for the correct execution of a transaction T:

Read O. Copy object O into T's local workspace. In case there is no timestamp associated with the object, set it to the current time $t(O,T) = $ Clock, which is an upper bound to the last time it was modified.

Validate T. For all objects O accessed by the transaction check in a *critical section* whether $t(O,T) > t(O)$.

- Abort T if the above condition is not true for *any* object.
- Otherwise commit T and externalize all objects O in the write set of the transaction, after setting $t(O) = Clock$.

Validation may be carried out in a *critical section,* such that the serialized validation process might constitute a bottleneck at high transaction volumes. In fact it is adequate to acquire temporary locks on all objects accessed by the transaction by an atomic action, which still introduces some serial processing. While validation is carried out at the completion of a transaction T, there may be a need to invoke it more frequently, e.g., at the time a transaction accesses an object or other instances of time based on transaction's resource consumption to ensure that transaction's execution is not wasteful. More frequent serialized processing for validation may introduce unacceptable delays and hence a more efficient validation scheme is required.

The alternative implementation uses *access entries,* which similarly to locks are appended to a list based on the hash class of the object, e.g., as determined by its address [GrRe92], signifying that a transaction T has accessed an object O. Access entries can be used at commit time to identify conflicted transactions and mark them as "injured". According to the *kill option* or *broadcast commit option* a transaction is aborted "right away",[32] while according to the *die option* or *silent commit* option an injured transaction is only aborted at the end of its execution [Robi84],[RyTh87]. No validation is required at the completion of the first execution phase of a transaction (i.e., end of its read phase) when a transaction is already injured; its access entries are deleted and the transaction is aborted. Otherwise, the following actions are taken as part of a transaction's commit processing:

1. The transaction locks all of its access entries by an atomic action, which is necessary to ensure serialization with respect to other transactions with conflicting accesses. If a transaction encounters a lock conflict at this point, it is simply delayed until the required access entries are unlocked. Note that a similar problem arises in the context of the hybrid concurrency control methods described in Section 5.4, which as part of transaction commit involves locking in the second phase.

2. The access entries of objects updated by the transaction are used to injure transactions which have accessed the objects.

3. The transaction writes its log records, externalizes updated objects by writing them out to the database buffer, and deletes access entries.

Aborted transactions can be restarted right away, since the conflicting transactions have left the system after committing, i.e., no further conflicts will occur. In some cases multiple transactions may be aborted by the same committing transaction, because of their access to the same object. Random delays are introduced in [AgCL87] to prevent further conflicts among aborted transactions, e.g., transactions updating the same object. Since this is expected to occur infrequently and given the difficulty of determining the duration of random delays, the following options are available: (i) restart aborted transactions immediately, which has the disadvantage of wasted processing; (ii) serialize the execution of aborted transactions when it is known that they conflict with each other, e.g., by updating the same object, (iii) information

---

[32] While this is implementation dependent, transaction abort is usually deferred until its next interaction with the concurrency control manager component of the DBMS. Otherwise the concurrency control manager needs to communicate with the resource managers of the system, e.g., to preempt it from the CPU or cancel its disk request.

about conflicting transaction requests can be used to schedule their execution to prevent conflicts (this is a generalization of (ii)).

The distinction between *backward-oriented* and *forward-oriented* optimistic concurrency control is made in [Haer84]. The backward-oriented optimistic concurrency control method corresponds to validation preceding commit, as described earlier. In forward-oriented optimistic concurrency control a transaction checks whether its write set conflicts with the read sets of transactions in their read phase and "the writesets are only propagated if they do not conflict with current readsets of all other active transactions." More generally, forward-oriented optimistic concurrency control provides opportunities for performance improvement as follows:

1. Defer transaction commit when there is a conflict. A case when deferring transaction validation results in a potentially improved performance is as follows. An object modified by the validated transaction has been read by another transaction. Deferring the introduction of the modified object into the database allows the other transaction to validate successfully. Note that this case can also be handled through versioning. Consider T_1 which is ready to commit having modified object O_A to $O_{A'}$. T_2, which is in its read phase, may have read O_A and used it to modify O_B to $O_{B'}$. Deferring T_1's commit to after T_2's commit results in the serialization order $T_2 \rightarrow T_1$.

2. A validating transaction which conflicts with other transactions may commit suicide, although it has not been injured earlier, since this action is expected to improve overall performance, e.g., by reducing wasted processing.

At this point we discuss approaches that can be used to exploit the performance improvement possible by deferred transaction commits[33] and suicides for validated transactions. The main concern here is minimizing transaction response time by reducing data contention as well as wasted processing. An attempt is made to achieve these two goals by aborting transactions holding fewer access entries which have also utilized less system resources than other transactions. The optimistic kill option is adopted here, since it is assumed that transaction re-executions incur the same cost as the original execution, as in the case of a main storage database. Consider a validated transaction T_2 which conflicts with T_1, which has not completed its execution. Let C_2 denote the processing cost of T_2 and C_1 the processing cost (so far) of T_1. If $C_2 > C_1$ then it is sensible from the viewpoint of reducing wasted processing to commit T_2 and to kill T_1. The choice is less clear if C_1 is much larger than C_2, since it is more advantageous from system's viewpoint for T_2 to commit suicide than for T_1 to be killed. However, T_1's suicide might

---

[33] This is for a different reason than item (1) in the above list, namely when both transactions have a need to update an object.

be in vain because the current execution of T_2 may not be successful after all. A possible approach in this case is to enter T_2 into a *pending state*. Thus if T_1 commits then T_2 is aborted and if T_1 aborts then T_2 can commit. Since we postulate that none of the transactions is very long, the delay introduced by deferring commits is not expected to result in an unacceptable increase in response time. On the other hand, a pending transaction is a "sitting duck", since it may be conflicted by other transactions.

As a continuation of the previous example consider a newly completed transaction T_3, which conflicts with T_1, which is still running. At this point T_1 will be killed if $C_2 + C_3 > C'_1$. Otherwise, if C'_1 is much larger than $C_2 + C_3$ then T_3 will also enter the pending state. Let us next consider a more complicated case when T_3 conflicts with both T_1 and T_2. If $C_3 > C'_1 + C_2$ then both T_1 and T_2 are killed and T_3 commits. Otherwise, T_3 enters the pending state.

The system state can be represented by a dependency graph [BCFP87] specifying the conflicts among transactions, e.g., $T_2 \rightarrow T_1 \leftarrow T_3$, for the last example. There are two types of transactions in the graph *pending* and *active*. Graphs are modified upon transaction completion and the graph reduction is in the form of transaction commits and aborts. The size of the dependency graph may grow at higher levels of data contention, hence heuristics are required to "optimize" system performance, while incurring a low overhead in reducing the graph. For example, one may only consider *immediate or distance of one conflicts*, i.e., transactions conflicted with a newly validated transaction, as well as transactions which had previously injured it nonfatally. This can be extended to immediate and distance of two conflicts.

Simulation experiments with variations of the above paradigm yielded little or no improvement in performance over the kill option. This is partially attributable to the fact that pending transactions are vulnerable to further conflicts, i.e., an initially successfully validated transaction may be injured and killed while it is in the pending state.

We next describe an optimistic concurrency control method which commits transactions in the order of the timestamps assigned to them upon their arrival to the system. A transaction T completing its execution

1. Commits if all conflicting transactions have a greater timestamp than T. The latter transactions are killed.

2. Dies if there are any conflicting transactions with a smaller timestamp and waits on the completion of those transactions.

It is needless to say that the performance of this method, which emulates the timestamp ordering method (see Section 6.1 in Chapter 6), is inferior to ordinary optimistic concurrency control.

A certification method based on *intervals of timestamps* [BCFP87] is described in Section 6.1 in Chapter 6.

5.3 Mechanisms Used by Two-Phase Processing Methods

In this section we describe mechanisms associated with transaction scheduling methods which take advantage of access invariance.

1. **Transaction phases.** A transaction phase corresponds to an instance of its execution. The first execution phase of a transaction, which may be unsuccessful, serves the role of priming the database buffer for transactions benefitting from access invariance. We only distinguish between executions in the first phase and further phases, since the execution in the first phase usually requires disk I/O, when access invariance prevails further execution phases do not require disk I/O and can be treated similarly from the scheduling viewpoint.

2. **Running modes.** We consider three running modes:

   a. *Virtual execution mode.* Virtual execution is used to determine the access pattern or script of a transaction with some degree of certainty. This is accomplished by running a transaction with no concurrency control, i.e., reading a stable version of uncommitted data or previously committed data if available, e.g., through versioning. It should be noted that transaction type and the input data to the transaction provides some information about the future behavior of a transaction, but there is usually a dependency on the state of the database, which is resolved via virtual execution.

   A "pipelined" transaction processing system is proposed in [Reut85], which uses all processors, but one, of a multiprocessor to prefetch data (effectively in virtual execution mode), while a dedicated processor *serially* re-executes transactions which have completed their first execution phase. It is suggested in [Reut85] that it should be possible to reduce pathlengths for second phase execution by specializing the software. For example, extra bits may be associated with objects in main storage to indicate their locking status [GMSa92], e.g., the first bit indicates that the object is locked in exclusive mode and the second bit that there is a pending transaction. In a prototype which implements a similar concept [LiNa88], only one thread in a multithreaded system carries out transaction updates, obviating the need for concurrency control. The two-phase processing methods described in Section 5.4 generalize the aforementioned pipelined transaction processing method [FrRT90],[FrRT92].

   b. *Optimistic mode.* The optimistic die or kill options can be used, but the die option is more suitable for the first phase and the kill option for further phases, provided that the transaction exhibits access invariance. Once it is known that a transaction cannot validate successfully, it is preferable to run the transaction in virtual execution mode, since it incurs less overhead.

c. *Locking mode.* The following possibilities exist: (i) the dynamic locking method; (ii) static locking or lock preclaiming is only possible in the second phase, since the locks required for transaction execution are identified in the first phase (provided that we have access invariance); (iii) the running priority or other wait depth limited methods may be also used, especially as a starting point in the first phase. An "aborted" transaction in this case releases its lock, but rather than being re-started, continues its execution in virtual execution mode.

Switching from a weaker to a stronger mode, such as virtual execution →optimistic concurrency control, virtual execution→locking, or optimistic concurrency control→locking is more difficult. Consider switching the running mode of a transaction from optimistic to locking, which is considered in [FrRT91a],[YuDa93] (see Section 5.4). Upgrading the access entries of a transaction to locks may result in other transactions being injured. In addition, depending on the implementation, transaction's updates may have to be externalized at this point.

3. **Locking priorities.** A two-phase processing method should specify how data conflicts are resolved [FrRT92]: (i) among transactions in the same phase; (ii) among transactions in different phases.

Locks are given a higher priority than access entries, since: (i) transactions in optimistic mode are much more susceptible to aborts than transactions with standard locking; (ii) the fact that the optimistic mode is used in the first phase, followed by the locking mode in further phases. We next consider lock conflicts.

- *No locking priorities.* Lock requests are handled in FCFS order, regardless of the phase of the transaction making the lock request.

- *Nonpreemptive locking priorities.* Lock requests by second phase transactions are given a higher priority than first phase transactions. This scheme is susceptible to starvation, because a first phase transaction may be repeatedly bypassed by second phase transactions.[34]

- *Preemptive locking priorities.* Lock requests by transactions in the second or further phases are given preemptive priority with respect to locks held by first phase transactions. There is less need to distinguish between the priorities of transactions in further phases, because the degree of concurrency for such transactions is small. A transaction which loses one (or more) of its locks due to preemption may be aborted or continue running in virtual execution mode. This decision

---

[34] This problem may be handled by increasing the priorities of bypassed locks in an appropriate manner, but this overly complicates the implementation.

is based on the phase of the transaction being aborted and whether it exhibits access invariance or not.

Preemptive lock priorities result in wasted CPU processing and also wasted lock utilization, but may reduce lock holding times and data contention, which may result in an improvement in effective throughput in a high data contention environment. With several first phase transactions enqueued for a lock, there is the choice of only aborting the transaction holding the lock or all transactions. The latter method, while resulting in more wasted processing, has the advantage of reducing transaction response time, provided adequate spare processing capacity is available.

Based on earlier simulation studies [FrRT92], only the last option will be considered in Section 5.4.

4. **Transaction spawning.** As an alternative to simply blocking a transaction when it encounters a lock conflict, it is possible to *spawn* a subtransaction [FrRT92]. The subtransaction will run in virtual execution mode, prefetching data required for the main transaction's execution. To ensure that the transaction can continue running from the point that it was blocked, a checkpoint is taken prior to spawning the subtransaction, which is provided with its private workspace.

5. **Checkpointing at the transaction level.** This type of checkpointing can be used to reduce the wasted processing due to transaction aborts. Checkpointing in optimistic concurrency control is discussed in Section 5.4.

6. **CPU priorities.** Phase two processing is prioritized with respect to phase one processing, in order to minimize the holding time for locks and access entries in this phase. Note also that the execution time in the first phase is dominated by disk I/O time and little is lost by lowering the CPU priority in this phase. The holding time of a lock or an access entry has a direct effect on the degree of data contention. Reducing the holding time of locks in the second phase reduces the probability of lock conflict among second phase transactions. Also reducing the holding time of access entries in this phase increases the chances of a successful validation in the second phase. It is therefore meaningful to provide second phase transactions a preemptive CPU priority with respect to first phase transactions.[35]

A first phase transaction runs at a lower priority in virtual execution mode, than in optimistic or locking mode. Transactions in the second phase have an even higher priority, regardless of their running mode, than transactions in the first phase, i.e., three priority levels are required: (i) highest

---

[35] Note that this system is not susceptible to the *priority inversion problem* [Rajk91], which arises when preemptive priorities are used to meet deadlines in a real-time system. A preempted low priority task (T_1) holding locks can be preempted at the CPU by a medium priority task (T_2), while blocking a high priority task (T_3). Several methods are proposed in [Rajk91] to resolve this problem, e.g., the *priority inheritance method* raises the priority of a blocked task to that of the highest priority task blocked by it.

priority for second phase transactions; (ii) intermediate priority for first phase transactions running in optimistic or locking mode; (iii) lowest priority for first phase transactions running in virtual execution mode.

5.3.1 Integrated Concurrency Control and CPU Scheduling

This paradigm is based on matching the number of executing transactions with the availability of hardware resources in the system, e.g., CPU utilization [FrRT91b]. For example, transactions in the system are prioritized based on whether they are runnable under: (1) standard locking, i.e., strict two-phase locking with the general waiting method; (2) running priority, which means transactions which are not runnable by the general waiting method, but runnable with the running priority method, e.g., transaction T_C in the waits for graph $T_C \rightarrow T_B \rightarrow T_A$; (3) the optimistic method, where all transactions are runnable. Transactions running according to 1, 2, and 3 maintain the same CPU priority (with 1 being the highest priority). When the CPU is underutilized (because there are no transactions such as T_A to run), the scheduler will first run transactions such as T_C. This seems to require the abort of T_B, but this is not required if a private workspace paradigm is adopted (T_C does not see T_B's updates as if it is aborted), which facilitates running in optimistic mode as well. If the CPU is still not fully utilized after running transactions such as T_C, the scheduler will run all transactions, including transactions such as T_B. Conversely, more conservative running options are adopted when the CPU is fully utilized. Further investigations are required to ascertain the viability of this method.

5.4 Description of Two-Phase Processing Methods

We specify transaction scheduling methods utilizing the mechanisms described in Section 5.3. The term two-phase rather than multiphase is used here, since most transactions complete their execution in two phases, although more than one transaction restart is possible in some cases. Virtual execution and the optimistic die option are suitable for the first execution phase, because they serve the purpose of prefetching data for the second execution phase. To reduce the variability of transaction response times, it is best to use a running mode in the second phase which does not allow repeated aborts, especially those caused by first phase transactions.

Data contention is less of a problem in the second phase than the first phase, since the mean number of transactions executing in this phase is a relatively small fraction of the total number. Consider transactions which in their first phase incur 20 msec. of CPU processing and nine disk accesses due to buffer misses (each disk I/O requires 20 msec.). The second phase only requires 20 msec. of CPU processing, which is one tenth of the time spent in the first phase (we assume that the above figures include queueing delays). It follows from Little's result (by multiplying the effective throughput for transactions by the time spent in the two phases) that there are ten times more transactions in the first phase than in the second phase. The fact that the increase in the number of transactions in the system is rather small, implies a rather small increase in main storage space requirements to hold the states of active transactions and the database buffer size, to maintain the hit ratio at the same level.

A list of viable two-phase processing methods is specified as $\phi_1/\phi_2 - \phi_3 - \phi_4 - \ldots$ where ϕ_1 is the concurrency control method used in phase 1 and ϕ_i, $i \geq 2$ is the concurrency control methods used in further phases. In case a transaction is aborted in ϕ_2, it is usually re-executed with the same concurrency control method, but this is not always the case, e.g., when it is discovered that access invariance is violated [ThRa90],[Thom92a]. Representative two-phase processing methods are as follows:

1. *Virtual execution/serialization- locking- optimistic kill.* Virtual execution followed by serialized execution is the method described in [Reut85], which is based on running transactions serially in the second phase, while the other methods allow concurrent transaction processing in this phase. The locking method in the second phase may be dynamic (on demand), but static locking is also possible, since the identities of locks are known provided access invariance prevails. An analysis for virtual execution/dynamic locking is provided in [ThRy91] and its effect on increasing the maximum throughput in a high data contention environment is quantified by a numerical example. The use of the optimistic kill versus the optimistic die option in the second phase is justified below.

2. *Optimistic die/kill.* The optimistic die option in the first phase is beneficial because it leads to data prefetching, but its repeated use in further phases is not justifiable, since it does not contribute to data prefetching. The optimistic kill option, which minimizes wasted processing is therefore suitable for the further phases.

   A successfully validated transaction in either phase may injure a transaction in the first or second phase. A forward-oriented optimistic concurrency control may be used to give preferential treatment to second phase transactions, i.e., by aborting first phase transactions in their validation phase which conflict with second phase transactions. While this approach potentially reduces the variability in transaction response times, simulation results show that it results in degraded performance. This is ascribable to the fact that a second phase transaction can still fail its validation. Note, however, that due to their longer processing time, first phase transactions are more susceptible to injury than second phase transactions.

3. *Optimistic kill/kill.* The kill method is beneficial in the first phase in the following cases: (i) transactions are not access invariant; (ii) the database is main storage resident or few disk accesses are required due to a high

buffer hit ratio; (iii) limited processing capacity, such that wasted processing cannot be tolerated. Thus running a transaction to the end to take advantage of access invariance is not beneficial in all cases. The above comments about transaction validation priorities also apply in this case.

4. *Optimistic die/locking.* These are examples of *hybrid* concurrency control methods. The advantage of hybrid concurrency control methods with respect to optimistic concurrency control is that second phase transactions can be given priority with respect to first phase transactions, i.e., lock requests conflicting with access entries result in the fatal injury of the corresponding first phase transaction. Note that when a standard locking method is in effect, a transaction in the second phase, which has injured a first phase transaction, may itself be aborted. However, this is expected to have a small effect on performance, since deadlocks are rare.

It should be noted that these policies reduce the variability of transaction response time with respect to the die/kill and kill/kill options, since transactions in the second phase are not affected by transactions in the first phase. This comment is also true for the method that follows.

5. *Running priority_virtual execution/locking.* While both the asymmetric running priority method and the symmetric running priority method are applicable, only the asymmetric running priority method is considered here for the sake of brevity. According to the running priority_virtual execution mode a transaction in the first phase may be aborted because it is blocked by another first phase transaction or due to lock preemption by a second phase transaction, since lock requests by transactions in the second phase have a preemptive priority with respect to locks held by first phase transactions. The first phase transaction copies objects protected by its locks into a private workspace, releases its locks (losing its access rights on the objects), but rather than being aborted it continues running in virtual execution mode. A first phase transaction (in running priority mode) is blocked when it has a lock conflict with an active or blocked second phase transaction, because lock requests by second phase transactions have a higher priority than first phase transactions.

When a transaction in the first phase (say T) is conflicted by a transaction T', which is also in the first phase or in general a transaction whose execution may be unsuccessful, although this transaction is in its second phase, then running T in optimistic die rather than virtual execution mode has the advantage that the transaction can attempt validation and may be successful if T' itself is conflicted. In effect T pretends to be killed, but it may recover at the cost of the aborted conflicting transactions (see similar discussion for optimistic die/locking method).

We will use this context to elaborate on transaction spawning at this point. A conflicted transaction (say T_i) takes a checkpoint at the point it was conflicted and then spawns a subtransaction, which continues running in virtual execution mode. There are two possibilities:

- T_i is unblocked before the spawned subtransaction completes its execution. There are two choices: (i) abort the spawned subtransaction; (ii) run the spawned subtransaction to the end, such that no spawning will be required if the transaction is blocked again.

- The spawned subtransaction completes while T_i is still blocked. In this case T_i is switched from the first to the second phase. In case T_i is blocked by a first phase transaction and provided that lock requests by second phase transactions have a preemptive priority with respect to first phase transactions, then the first phase transaction is aborted releasing its locks. If T_i is blocked by a second phase transaction, it will remain blocked until this transaction completes.

  Preliminary simulation results have shown that transaction spawning does not lead to a significant improvement in performance with respect to the running priority-virtual execution/locking two-phase processing method [FrRT92]. More recently transaction spawning has been considered in the context of real-time transactions [BeBr95].

The *branching transaction paradigm* differs from transaction spawning in that when a lock conflict occurs, it allows transaction branching based on the old and new value of the locked variable [BuTh94]. This method is motivated by massively parallel computers and is presented in the context of multiversion two-phase locking. "Branch restriction policies" are required, since otherwise the number of transactions in the system grows exponentially leading to thrashing (due to resource exhaustion).

The *polyvalues method* [Mont78], intended for coping with failures in a distributed database environment, provides a similar capability through a bookkeeping tool, which keeps track of several potential values for a data item depending on the commit or abort of precommitted transactions [CePe84],[GrRe92]. For example, when two pending transactions T_1 and T_2 have accessed a bank balance, there are three polyvalues: $(Balance_{init} - Withdraw_1 - Withdraw_2, T_1, T_2)$, $(Balance_{init} - Withdraw_1, T_1, \neg T_2)$, and $(Balance_{init} - Withdraw_2, \neg T_1, T_2)$, where T_i (respectively $\neg T_i$) indicates the commit (respectively abort) of transaction T_i, respectively. Thus items remaining locked due to the failure of a commit coordinator can be accessed conditionally by other transactions. Note that branching is unnecessary for transactions which just require the balance to exceed a certain value. The escrow paradigm generalizes and formalizes polyvalues in the case of aggregate data [ONei86] (see Section 3.6 in Chapter 3).

The issue of accessing old or new values arises in the context of hybrid concurrency control methods as well. Alternative implementations of the optimistic die/static locking two-phase processing method are discussed in [ThRa90],[Thom92a]:

1. Always access committed data. In case there is a second phase transaction holding a lock on an object then its value in the database buffer may be uncommitted. To ensure that the database buffer only holds committed data, the private workspace paradigm for optimistic concurrency control should be also followed for the locking mode.[36] This option leads to the abort of the transaction accessing the object locked in exclusive mode, unless the transaction holding the lock is aborted.

2. Allow access to modified but uncommitted data, which is possible if objects locked in exclusive mode are written directly onto the database buffer, since pointers to access data in the private workspace may be unavailable.

   A transaction which has locked an object in exclusive mode may or may not have modified it in its second execution phase or may modify it again, such that this may or may not be an up-to-date version of the object. In fact the version of an object is determined by the timestamp assigned to it at transaction commit time. Earlier assignment of timestamps to objects, which are no longer to be updated by the locking transaction is an option that is expected to yield improved performance, since it allows other transactions *earlier access to possibly up-to-date version of the object,* but on the negative side it introduces complications and may lead to cascading aborts if the transaction is aborted (similar concepts are discussed in Section 3.6 in Chapter 3 [JaSh92],[AEAL94],[SGMS94]).

3. Block access until the exclusive lock is released, which is not truly an "optimistic" approach to data access.

The latter two policies can be best implemented with access entries. The second method is expected to yield the best performance. There is little difference between the performance attained by the first and third methods, as was observed from the simulation results of a distributed optimistic concurrency control method with the optimistic die option in the first phase and lock preclaiming in the second phase [Thom92a].

5.4.1 Performance Comparison of Two-Phase Processing Methods

We summarize here the conclusions from simulation results in [FrRT90],[FrRT92], as well as the conclusions in [ThRy86],[AgCL87]. The comparison of concurrency control methods is based on their effective throughput characteristic $(T(M), M \geq 1$. The system throughput characteristic $(t(M), M \geq 1)$, which is an *upper bound* to the effective throughput characteristic, can be obtained by postulating shared lock requests in the simulation.

---

[36] Alternatively, the before-images [GrRe92] of the modified object should be accessed from the log, which can be done efficiently only if the object is available in main storage.

1. The virtual execution/locking method provides a *lower bound* to the effective throughput characteristic attainable by two-phase processing methods. There is little difference between the performance attained by the dynamic locking and static locking methods in the second phase, since there are few transactions in this phase at any time and little lock contention. Static locking is preferable to dynamic locking in that it prevents transaction aborts due to deadlocks. In a high data contention system with adequate hardware resources the virtual execution/locking method outperforms standard locking [ThRy91].

2. The optimistic die/kill method outperforms the optimistic kill/kill method in a system with adequate hardware resources and access invariance, but this is not so in a system with limited hardware resources [FrRT90], [FrRT92]. This is because executing transactions to the end (almost) ensures their successful re-execution in the first case, since transaction re-execution time without disk I/O tends to be very short. The optimistic kill/kill method also benefits from the prefetching effect up to the point it was aborted, while wasting less CPU processing than the optimistic die/kill method.

3. The optimistic die/kill method outperforms the running priority-virtual execution/locking method in high contention systems with adequate hardware resources and vice-versa. The main reason is that the latter method is more conservative than the first method in the first execution phase and it reduces wasted processing by allowing conflicted transactions to wait.

An important observation about two-phase processing methods is that their performance follows almost the same pattern at high levels of transaction concurrency, as determined by the saturation of the bottleneck hardware resource. This is because few of the transactions can commit successfully at the end of their first execution phase and wasted processing leads to an early saturation of hardware resources. In high data contention systems requiring disk I/O and with adequate hardware resources two-phase processing methods can outperform the WDL method [FrRT92]. However, this is not always so, e.g., the WDL method outperforms the optimistic die/static locking method in a system with a main storage database with a large number of processors [FrRT92]. On the other hand, the WDL method is outperformed by the more efficient optimistic kill option in this case.

The performance of two-phase processing methods can be improved by utilizing adaptive methods which minimize the additional (or wasted) processing, when the processors are saturated, i.e., fully utilized. One such method is to initially run transactions according to the optimistic die/kill method and switch to the running priority_virtual execution/locking method when the processors become saturated due to the increased load as more transactions are activated [FrRT91a]. When the running priority_virtual execution/locking method saturates the processors, a more conservative method can be adopted by aborting a blocked transaction only when it is blocking $b \geq 2$ transactions, instead of one (this concept was also discussed in the context of an adaptive running priority method in Section 4.1 in Chapter 4, where b is referred to transaction's breadth). The value of b can be gradually increased, until the processors are no longer saturated, but still highly utilized. This ensures that the wasted processing in the system is minimized and the useful processing (and hence the effective throughput) is maximized. We report on the results of a simulation study to quantify this effect: fixed size transactions with $K = 16$, $D = 32000$, with 1000 hot-spots, 25% accesses to hot-spots, and a 50% hit ratio for cold-spots,[37] four 25 MIPS processors, and transaction path-lengths as given in [FrRT92]. The optimistic method is observed to provide the highest throughput at $M = 50$ and as the multiprogramming level is increased, the maximum throughput with the running priority_virtual execution/locking method is obtained at $b = 1, 2, 3$ at $M = 60, 75, 100$, respectively. The improvement in throughput from optimistic die/kill to asymmetric running priority with $b \geq 2$ is approximately 10% at $M = 75$.

We next revisit the method in Section 5.3, which switches transactions directly from optimistic mode to locking mode. This method is advantageous from the performance viewpoint, since the vulnerability of a transaction running in optimistic mode to being injured increases as it nears its completion, which is due the quadratic effect [FrRT92] (see Section 5.5). The method in [YuDa93] switches fixed size transactions of size K from optimistic die mode to locking mode at $K' < K$, where K' is determined by a heuristic based on the utilization of the bottleneck resource (the CPU) and the probability of lock conflict (P_c). A transaction encountering a disk I/O after switching modes may incur long lock holding times, which may increase the level of lock contention. Simulation results show an improvement in performance when transactions exhibit access invariance with respect to the die/kill method [YuDa93]. This method is not easily extensible to multiple transaction classes, because of the difficulty of determining the appropriate switching points for different transaction classes. In addition it is more difficult to predict transaction sizes when multiple transactions are involved.

5.4.2 Checkpointing in Optimistic Concurrency Control

The effect of checkpointing (or volatile savepoints [GrRe92]) at the level of individual transactions are investigated in the context of the optimistic kill option [Thom95d].[38] Checkpointing is more appropriate to optimistic concurrency control than restart-oriented locking methods, since: (i) it solely uses aborts to resolve data conflicts; (ii) checkpointing might be facilitated by the private

---

[37] Since the hot-spots always reside in the database buffer, the buffer hit ratio for the first execution phase of transactions is 62.5%.

[38] Specifying just one method, implies its repetition in further phases.

workspace paradigm. There is a tradeoff between checkpointing overhead and the saved processing due to *partial rollbacks*, which allows a transaction to resume execution from the checkpoint preceding the data item to be released.

Checkpointing is observed not to be effective at high contention levels, if the database objects are uniformly accessed, even if checkpointing cost is low such that checkpoints can be taken before accessing each object. This is because the probability with which a data object is conflicted is proportional to the length of time since it was accessed (see discussion in Section 5.5), such that objects accessed at the beginning of transaction execution are more vulnerable than those accessed towards its completion. In case only one checkpoint is to be taken, it follows from numerical results in [Thom95d], that it is best to take the checkpoint after one third of objects required by a transaction are accessed (note that this number may not be known a priori), which implies that at most 1/3 of a transaction's processing can be saved. Performance can be improved if accesses to hot-spots are deferred to the end of transaction execution and a checkpoint is taken prior to that point, because: (i) objects held for a short duration of time are less vulnerable to conflicts; (ii) most of the processing acquired by the transaction is preserved if a data conflict occurs.

5.5 Performance Analysis of Optimistic Concurrency Control Methods

Analytic solution methods to evaluate the performance of optimistic concurrency control methods and insights gained from these analyses are outlined in this section. An analysis of a two-phase processing method with virtual execution in the first phase appears in [ThRy91] and is similar to the analysis in Section 3.2 in Chapter 3 with an appropriately long first step. We also outline the analysis of a hybrid concurrency control method at the end of this section.

One key observation which can be demonstrated by a rather simple analysis is that there is an increase in the frequency of aborts with transaction size [RyTh87], which is referred to as the *quadratic effect* [FrRT92]. Thus when transactions steps have equal processing times, the probability of conflict with an optimistic die (respectively kill) option increases proportionally to k^2/D (respectively $k^2/(2D)$). This effect is also noted in [RyTh87], where it is observed from numerical results that the wasted processing in a system with variable transaction sizes is dominated by the largest transaction sizes.

5.5.1 An Analytic Solution for Optimistic Concurrency Control

The first paper dealing with the analysis of optimistic concurrency control considers the die option with static data access, i.e., all objects required by a transaction are accessed at the beginning of transaction execution [MeNa82]. Transactions arrive according to a Poisson process (with rate λ) to a computer system which can process at most M_{max} transactions at a time. A hierarchical solution method is adopted (see Section 2.4 in Chapter 2), where a 2-dimensional Markov chain at the higher-level is only concerned with transaction arrivals and departures. For state $S_{i,j}$, i denotes the number of transactions in the system and j the number of transactions that can complete successfully. Note that $i \geq 0$, $0 \leq j \leq M_{max}$ and $j \leq i$.

The transition rates at the higher level model are based on transaction throughputs obtained by solving the queueing network model of the underlying computer system at the lower level model (using methods described in Section 2.3 in Chapter 2). The analysis at this level also takes into account the fact that bad (previously conflicted) transactions will fail their validation upon completion. The probability that a transaction needs re-execution is $1 - u$, where u is obtained from the higher-level model as the ratio of the mean number of transactions that can complete successfully and all transactions.[39]

The probability of a data conflict in a database with size D when the committing (respectively conflicting) transaction is updating m (respectively accessing n) data objects, which are accessed with uniform probabilities, is given by: $\phi(n,m) = 1 - \binom{D-n}{m} / \binom{D}{m} \simeq 1 - (1 - n/D)^m \simeq nm/D$. In the case of fixed size transactions with size k and with all k accessed objects updated is $\psi = \phi(k,k) \simeq k^2/D$. A different expression is applicable when the lock requests are sequential [RyTh87]. The transition rates of the Markov chain are affected by the probability that a committing transaction at $S_{k,j}$ conflicts with l transactions from the remaining $j-1$ transactions is given by the binomial distribution $\binom{j-1}{l} \psi^l (1 - \psi)^{j-1-l}$.

The mean number of transactions in the system ($\overline{M}_{sys}$) and u are obtained by solving the state equilibrium equations. The mean transaction response time is $R = \overline{M}_{sys}/\lambda$. Given that the number of states in the first dimension is infinite, the system capacity (the number of transactions that can be held in the system) is selected such that these equations can be solved at a reasonable cost, while the fraction of rejected transactions remains negligibly small. A complication of this analytical solution is that u required by the analysis of the lower level model is computed at the higher level model, which results in an iterative solution based on u as its convergence criterion.

---

[39] Since u is an average over all possible states, it underestimates (respectively overestimates) the abort rate at states with few (respectively many) activated transactions. Further investigation is required to determine if decomposing the higher level analysis into a layer with a fixed number of transactions M and varying M in a higher level birth-death model (as in [Thom85],[RyTh90a]), would yield more accurate results in this respect.

Chapter 5: Two-Phase Processing Methods   105

The above analysis is shown to be quite accurate through validation against simulation results for up to 75% utilization, but overestimates performance at higher CPU utilizations. It is also observed from numerical results that the static locking method outperforms the optimistic die option, but the improvement in response time is rather small at low lock contention levels.

5.5.2 An Improved Analysis of Optimistic Concurrency Control

As explained in [MoWo85] the analysis in [MeNa82] underestimates the mean response times for the optimistic concurrency control method at higher levels of data contention. The Markov chain model at the higher level of the analysis assumes that transaction processing times are exponentially distributed. It is implicit in the Markov chain analysis that the transaction processing times are resampled when the transaction is aborted and restarted. Thus the static optimistic concurrency control method successfully validates instances of transaction execution with shorter processing times, because there is a higher probability of success. The mean processing time of completed transactions is less than the mean processing time of the original transactions.

The analysis in [Mena82] is repeated in [MoWo84],[MoWo85], except that a closed system with M transactions is considered to simplify the discussion ([MoWo84] allows shared as well as exclusive accesses). Transaction processing times are assumed to be exponentially distributed with a mean $1/\mu$. The processing rate (system throughput) of a system with M transactions is $t(M) = \mu s(M)$, where $s(M)$ reflects the increased throughput due to transaction concurrency, but takes into account the degradation due to queueing effects. Let u denote the system efficiency [RyTh87] or the fraction of time the system is doing useful work. Then the transaction completion rate is $T(M) = ut(M) = u\mu s(M)$ and each transaction in the system sees other transactions committing with a rate $\lambda = (1 - 1/M)u\mu s(M)$. A key assumption used in this and further analyses is that *running transactions observe the commits of other transactions as a Poisson process* (with rate λ). The rate at which a transaction is conflicted is then $\gamma = \lambda\psi$, where ψ was obtained in Section 5.5.1.

The probability of a data conflict for a transaction with processing time x is $q = 1 - e^{-\gamma x M/s(M)}$. Provided that the execution time of a transaction remains fixed (at x), i.e., the execution time is not resampled when the transaction restarts, the number of times the transaction is executed in the system follows a geometric distribution $P_j = q(1 - q)^{j-1}$, $j \geq 1$ with a mean $\bar{J}(x) = 1/q = e^{\gamma x M/s(M)}$.

The system efficiency is defined as the ratio of the mean execution time of a transaction and its residence time in the system, which can be expressed as

$$u = \frac{E[xM/s(M)]}{E[xMe^{\gamma xM/s(M)}/s(M)]} = \frac{\int_0^{\infty} xe^{-\mu x}dx}{\int_0^{\infty} xe^{-(\mu - \gamma M/s(M))x}dx} = [1 - (M-1)\psi u)]^2,$$

$\gamma M/s(M) < \mu$ is required for the integral in the denominator to converge.[40] Solving the quadratic equation yields one acceptable root: $u = (1 + 2a - \sqrt{1 + 4a})/4a^2 \simeq 1 - 2a$, where $a = (M-1)\psi$ is small, such that higher terms in the expansion of $(1 + 4a)^{1/2}$ can be ignored.

As far as the relative performance of static locking and optimistic die is concerned, it is shown that static locking (with the FCFS with skip option in Section 3.3), which does not introduce any wasted processing outperforms the optimistic die option. The more efficient optimistic kill option (with object pre-claiming) is shown to have a performance indistinguishable from static locking in a system with infinite resources in [ThRy86]. The reader is referred to Section 5.4.1 for a more realistic performance comparison of optimistic concurrency control and locking methods.

5.5.3 Extensions of Analysis to Optimistic Kill Policy with Dynamic Accesses

This analysis is extended in several directions in [RyTh87]. Firstly, different distributions for the processing time are considered. Numerical investigations with the fixed, uniform, Erlang-$n + 1$ (where n is the number of assessed objects) and exponential distributions showed that u has its highest (respectively lowest) value when the processing times are fixed (respectively exponential) and that Erlang distribution outperforms the uniform distribution in most considered cases. Thus ignoring the effect of the variability of processing times results in overestimating performance.

The analysis in [RyTh87] also considers dynamic object accesses and the optimistic kill option. This analysis with static accesses and exponential processing times yields $u = (1 + a)^{-1} \simeq 1 - a$, which indicates that *the die option is twice as inefficient as the kill option*, with other parameters being the same. The analysis with dynamic data access differs from static access in that the conflict rate for different steps varies according to the number of data objects that have been accessed.

Multiple transaction classes, where transaction class is determined by its size, are additionally considered in [RyTh87]. An outline of the analysis in [RyTh87] is given here for the case of a closed system with M transactions and

---

[40] In effect the analysis in [MeNa92] assumes that the number of transaction executions ($\tilde{J}$) is independent from transaction execution time ($\tilde{X}$) and hence $E(\tilde{J}\tilde{X}) = \bar{J}\bar{X}$, which is not true in this case.

K classes with frequencies f_k, $1 \leq k \leq K$. The processing times of transactions in C_k, $1 \leq k \leq K$ are given by their probability density functions $b_k(x)$, $1 \leq k \leq K$. The effect of hardware resource contention is taken into account by expanding the processing times according to a function $\eta(M)$, which is obtainable by analyzing the computer system model and affects all transaction classes equally: $b_k(x|M) = b_k(x/\eta(M))/\eta(M)$, $1 \leq k \leq K$. The mean processing time for transactions in C_k at a degree of concurrency M is $R_k^e(M) = \eta(M)b_k$. The mean overall transaction response time is $R^a(M) = \sum_{c=1}^{c} f_k R_k^e(M)$. The system throughput is $T^a(M) = M/R^a(M)$.

The mean response time of a transaction in C_k is given by $R_k(M) = R_k^e(M) + R_k^w(M)$, where $R_k^w(M)$ denotes the wasted time due to transaction aborts. The mean overall response time is $R(M) = \sum_{k=1}^{K} f_k R_k(M)$, from which the effective throughput follows as $T(M) = M/R(M)$. The system efficiency is $U(M) = R^a(M)/R(M) = T(M)/T^a(M)$. Given $U(M)$ we have, $T(M) = U(M)T^a(M)$ and the per class throughputs are $T_k(M) = f_k T(M)$. The mean number of transactions in different classes is $\overline{M}_k = T_k(M)R_k(M)$.

The efficiency for transactions in C_k is $U_k(M) = R_k^e(M)/R_k(M)$, which is related to $U(M)$.

$$U(M) = \frac{R^a(M)}{R(M)} = \frac{R^a(M)}{\sum_{k=1}^{K} f_k R_k(M)} = \frac{R^a(M)}{\sum_{k=1}^{K} f_k R_k^a(M)/U_k(M)} \tag{5.1}$$

The solution method proceeds as follows. The rate of conflict for transactions in C_k is $\sigma_k(M) = (1 - 1/M)\, T(M)\, \psi_k$, where $\psi_k = \sum_{j=1}^{K} \phi(n_j, n_k) f_j$ with n_k denoting the number of objects accessed by C_k transactions. Taking into account the expansion in transaction processing time, we have

$$\gamma_k = \eta(M)\sigma_k(M) = \frac{(M-1)\psi_k}{b}\, U(M), \tag{5.2}$$

where $b = \sum_{k=1}^{K} b_k f_k$ is the mean processing time over all classes. The mean transaction residence time conditioned on its processing time being x (when it is executed singly) is $R_k(M|x) = \eta(M)xe^{\gamma_k x}$. Unconditioning and adopting the Laplace transform notation (see e.g., [Klei75]) for the sake of conciseness, we have:

$$R_k(M) = \int_0^\infty R_k(M|x)b_k(x)dx = \eta(M)\int_0^\infty xe^{\gamma_k x}dx = -\eta(M)B_k^{(1)}(-\gamma_k), \quad (5.3)$$

where the superscript (1) denotes the first derivative. The efficiency for transactions in C_k is then

$$U_k(M) = \frac{R_k^a(M)}{R_k(M)} = \frac{B_k^{(1)}(0)}{B_k^{(1)}(-\gamma_k)}. \quad (5.4)$$

Briefly, the iterative solution method proceeds as follows. Set $U(M) = 1$; obtain $T(M) = U(M)T^a(M)$; for classes $1 \leq k \leq K$ using equations (5.2), (5.3), and (5.4) to compute γ_k, $R_k(M)$, and $U_k(M)$, respectively; use equation (5.1) to compute $U(M)$ and check its value for convergence. If convergence has not been attained, iterate with the new value of $U(M)$. Arguments for the convergence of the iteration appear in [RyTh87].

The analysis can be easily modified to take into account the variability in transaction processing times across executions, e.g., due to the prefetching effect of a first execution phase [RyTh87].

5.5.4 The Analysis of a Hybrid Concurrency Control Method

We consider the optimistic die/static locking method, which is a representative concurrency control method. We postulate that first phase transactions access only committed data (according to item (1) at the end of Section 5.4). The analysis of the first phase, based on dynamic accesses to objects, can be accomplished using an appropriate method in [RyTh87]. This yields the probability that a transaction fails its validation (say P_{repeat}) and has to repeat its execution with static locking. The analysis of the second phase is simplified by assuming that transactions in this phase do not conflict with each other, but in case the lock conflict level is not negligible the analysis in [TayY87] (see Section 3.3) can be used for this purpose. Noting that transactions can be aborted only once, the increase in mean transaction response time can be expressed as $R(M) = r(M) + P_{repeat}r'(M)$, where the execution time in the second phase ($r'(M)$) is much smaller than $r(M)$. Starting with the initialization $P_{repeat} = 0$, the throughput is $T(M) = M/r(M)$, where $r(M)$ is the mean execution time in the first phase. The high value of $T(M)$ results in overestimating P_{repeat}, such that $T(M) = M/R(M)$ is underestimated. This results in also underestimating P_{repeat}, such that $T(M)$ is overestimated again, but to a smaller degree than before. This iteration converges in a few cycles. Analytic solutions for hybrid methods with fixed size transactions are also provided in [YuDL93].

CHAPTER 6: DISTRIBUTED DATABASES

The literature on concurrency control in distributed databases and their performance is vast and this section is intended to expose the reader to some of the key issues in this area. For more detailed discussions the reader is referred to [BeGo81],[Date83],[CePe84],[BeHG87],[CeGM88],[GrRe92]. We also point out how some of the previously discussed concurrency control methods can be extended to a distributed environment. In what follows we first discuss concurrency control methods for distributed databases, followed by their modeling and performance evaluation. A brief discussion of data-sharing and multidatabase systems follows.

6.1 Concurrency Control Methods for Distributed Databases

Standard locking (two-phase locking with the general waiting policy) is the prevalent concurrency control method in distributed databases. Database calls by a transaction running at one of the nodes of a distributed database are processed locally or remotely, depending on the location of referenced data, as determined by the database catalog or directory [Date83],[CePe84]. Distributed databases are mainly relational, because of the suitability of this model for data distribution, e.g., through horizontal data partitioning of a large table [Date83],[CePe84]. The processing of complex queries requires extensive optimizations, primarily to minimize the volume of data to be transmitted among the nodes of the distributed system [Date83],[CaPa84], but this is of little concern here since we are interested in the processing of short online transactions.

Deadlock detection is a major problem in distributed locking and numerous algorithms have therefore been proposed for this purpose [Knap87]. A problem with the so-called "path-pushing deadlock detection methods", which transmit local waits-for graphs to other nodes to detect global deadlocks by "gluing" local waits-for graphs together is that they are incorrect: (i) by not finding global deadlocks; (ii) detecting phantom deadlocks; (iii) both [Knap87]. Timeouts are one method to cope with this problem [JeTK89], even in shared-nothing systems (message passing multicomputers).

The timestamp ordering method is appropriate to distributed databases, since data conflicts can be resolved locally, without requiring additional messages), based on timestamps assigned to them at the beginning of their execution [CePe84],[BeHG87],[CeGM88]. Timestamps are drawn from a totally ordered domain [BeHG87], i.e., timestamps are unique monotonically increasing functions of time. Techniques to ensure uniqueness in a distributed system are discussed in [CePe84]. A transaction can successfully read (respectively update) an object if transaction's timestamp precedes object's update timestamp (respectively read and update timestamp) and otherwise the transaction is aborted and restarted with a new timestamp (the read timestamp of an object is the minimum of the timestamps of transactions which read it, while the update timestamp is that of the transaction which last updated it). The basic timestamp ordering method may result in *cascading aborts,* because the updates of uncommitted transactions are exposed to others [Sing91]. The variant of the timestamp ordering method considered in [ThRy86],[RyTh90b] (also see Section 5.2) does not have this property, but still has inferior performance with respect to other concurrency control methods.[41] Other variants of timestamp ordering methods are described in [CePe84],[CeGM88]. The reader is referred to [CeGM88],[Sing91] for performance analyses of this method.

The wound-wait method and the wait-die method (described in Section 4.1 in Chapter 4), while being based on locking, also rely on timestamps to resolve lock conflicts [RoSL78]. They are suited for a system with a low lock contention level and high costs for inter-node messages, which makes distributed deadlock detection costly. The WDL method [FrRT92] (see Chapter 4) also prevents deadlocks, but incurs more messages than the wound-wait method and the wait-die method [FHRT93]. *Two-phase commit* is required (regardless of the concurrency control method) to ensure transaction atomicity [Date83], [CePe84],[GrRe92], incurring additional messages and increased lock holding time. Minimizing the number of messages required for two-phase commit is the topic of [SBCM95]. Different data allocation schemes which minimize the number of messages and the need for global concurrency control are pertinent to replicated databases [CHKS91].

A large number of distributed optimistic concurrency control methods have been proposed [BCFP87],[CeGM88],[ThRa90],[CaLi89],[CaLi91]. A key problem in correctly implementing a distributed optimistic concurrency control method is to ensure that the validation of a transaction is carried out in the same order at all relevant nodes, e.g., by using global timestamps.

The hybrid optimistic concurrency control method in Section 5.4 in Chapter 5, with the optimistic die mode in the first phase and lock preclaiming in the second phase, is extended to a distributed hybrid optimistic concurrency control method in [ThRa90],[Thom92a]. A key feature of the hybrid optimistic concurrency control method is the combination of validation and two-phase commit messages. *Commit duration locking* ensures that the second phase of transaction execution, which is necessary if the transaction fails validation, is always successful because data blocks accessed by the transaction cannot

---

[41] The actions taken upon a data conflict of the timestamp ordering and the no-waiting method [TaSG85] (discussed in Chapter 4) are compared in [RyTh90b], where it is shown that the no-waiting method outperforms the timestamp ordering method, because the timestamp ordering method either takes the same action as the no-waiting method or aborts a transaction abort, while the no-waiting method does not.

be invalidated by others. Alternative implementations of hybrid optimistic concurrency control from the viewpoint of access to locked data, as discussed in Section 5.4 in Chapter 5, are investigated. Also discussed is the suitability of various implementations with and without access invariance. The number of messages generated by this method is the same as locking, but if caching of remote data is allowed, lock requests for remote objects cached locally can be deferred by combining them with two-phase commit messages. This method outperforms standard locking in high performance systems with higher levels of data contention, as would be expected from similar results in a centralized system.

The distributed validation method based on *intervals of timestamps* in [BCFP87] is worthy of mention.[42] At validation time a transaction gets a unique timestamp that determines its position in the serialization order, which, however, need not correspond to the validation order, so that transaction "numbers" need not be monotonically increasing. To derive a valid timestamp, time intervals are maintained for active transactions. At BOT (beginning of transaction), the interval is infinite $[0, \infty)$ and is reduced for each object access according to the object's read and write timestamps (denoted by RTS and WTS). If the interval is nonempty at EOT (end of transaction), transaction's success is guaranteed and the transaction timestamp can be chosen from the interval. Furthermore, the accessed objects RTS and WTS are adapted according to the newly assigned transaction timestamp and the time intervals of active transactions are adapted.

To illustrate this method, consider the following schedule of three transactions T_1, T_2, and T_3.

$r_3(x), r_2(x), w_3(y), w_1(x), r_2(y), c_1, c_2, c_3,$

where $r_i(x)$ (respectively $w_i(x)$) is the reading (respectively writing) of object x by T_i and c_i indicates T_i's completion. In standard backward-oriented optimistic concurrency control validation (see Section 5.2 in Chapter 5) T_3 and T_2 get aborted, since they have accessed old versions of object x. If we assume $RTS(x) = WTS(x) = 17$ and $RTS(y) = WTS(y) = 32$, we get the following time intervals after operation $r_2(y)$: $T_1:(17, \infty)$; $T_2:(32, \infty)$; $T_3:(32, \infty)$. If T_1's timestamp is set to 18, it would not be possible for T_2 and T_3 to get lower transaction number so that we would have to abort them. By setting T_1's transaction number say to 50, we get $WTS(x) = 50$. This modified object timestamp must be used to reduce the time intervals of running transactions, because they have not seen this new version. There are the following intervals $T_2:(32,50)$; $T_3:(32,50)$. Next T_3 can successfully commit, say with a transaction number 41. This leads to $RTS(x) := 41; WTS(y) := 41$ and a reduced time in-

---

[42] This material is based on an example contributed by Prof. Erhard Rahm from the Computer Science Department at University of Leipzig, Germany.

terval for T_2 (32,41). Finally T_2 can successfully commit, say with transaction number 37. The serialization order is $T_2(37) < T_3(41) < T_1(50)$, while the transaction completion and validation order was T_1, T_3, T_2.

6.1.1 Modeling and Performance Evaluation of Concurrency Control Methods in Distributed Databases

The complexity of the algorithm, i.e., the number of remote messages, is an important factor in assessing a distributed concurrency control method, since cost per message tends to be quite high [Gray88]. Thus some studies use the number of messages exchanged in comparing distributed concurrency control methods [BeGo81],[FHRT93].

The number of messages is also of interest in a *mobile computing environment* [ImBa94], where efficiency is determined by the number of transmissions from a mobile node, i.e., energy management of the battery. The *fractional data allocation* method allocates tokens to nodes based on anticipated demand, which can then be disposed of with no external coordination [Thom94b]. A brief review of related schemes also appears in [Thom94b] and [RaCh96], which is as follows [Kuma90],[SoSh90],[BaGM92],[KuSt92]. A preliminary investigation of the performance of the fractional data allocation method appears in [GoTh92]. The correctness criterion in replicated databases is *one copy serializability*, i.e., the interleaved execution of concurrent transactions is equivalent to serialzability on a single copy of the database [BeHG87]. *Epsilon-serializability* [PuLe92] and the *bounded ignorance* methods [KrBe94] allow some data inconsistency to attain higher performance.

To determine the more usual performance measures in traditional distributed databases, such as mean transaction response times for a given transaction throughput, the computer system model and the characteristics of the communication network should be specified, since the associated delays affect transaction response time.

The performance of a distributed database is affected by the transaction processing paradigm:

1. *Data request shipping* in the context of CICS (Customer Information Control System) [Date93] (or database call shipping [YCDT89]) involves making remote database calls, when the referenced data is not locally available. When the distributed database is relational, the best strategy to access distributed objects is determined by the query optimizer and is handled through database calls to appropriate nodes [Date83],[CePe84].

2. A node requiring access to remote data invokes an appropriate procedure at the remote node [CePe84], which is referred to as *distributed transaction processing* in CICS (Customer Information Control System) terminology [Date83]. This approach in the form of "stored procedures" is currently

available in some centralized DBMSs for improved performance by reducing database call overhead, since a stored procedure usually contains multiple database calls. The performance gains are higher in a distributed database environment, but this is at the cost of the loss of "location transparency" [Date83], i.e., re-allocation of data in the distributed system requires modifications to programs.

3. Request data pages from other nodes for local processing, referred to as *I/O request shipping* [YCDT89]. This approach off-loads the node holding the data from the associated processing. It is shown in [YCDT89] that in a system with high bandwidth interconnects this approach outperforms data request shipping at higher processor utilizations. This is attributable to the fact that in spite of the wasted communication bandwidth (since not all of the data on a page is required by the transaction), there is an improvement in performance by processing additional low level IMS database commands locally on prefetched data.

This method is used in *data sharing systems* where for improved performance blocks of data are sent directly from one system to another rather than to/from disk. This approach also fits the distributed shared virtual memory paradigm [BlBu93].

Transaction parallelism in distributed [CaLi89] and especially parallel databases i.e., shared nothing database machines, is an important consideration, which is related to multilevel transactions [WeHa93]. Note that the reduction in lock holding time, resulting from reduced transaction response time due to parallelism, may lead to improved performance when data contention is a factor.

The relative performance of distributed concurrency control methods is not as well understood as centralized concurrency control methods, but some of the insights gained from performance studies of centralized systems are applicable to distributed systems. A survey of earlier simulation and analytic studies appears in [Sevc83], which also provides formulas applicable to analyzing the performance of distributed database systems. The number of such studies is relatively small because of the complexity of distributed systems. Simplifying assumptions are usually used, e.g., a fully replicated database, fully interconnected network, network delays represented as $M/M/1$ queues, etc. The reader is referred to [NaMe84],[JeKT88],[RMRR92] for representative analytic studies.

Simulation is the main performance evaluation tool for distributed databases. Two comprehensive simulation studies of concurrency control methods appear in [CaLi89],[CaLi91]. The latter study varies the degree of file replication (using the *read-one, write-all* protocol, when appropriate) and compares the performance of two-phase locking and "optimistic" two-phase locking, which defers remote lock requests to commit time, the wound-wait method, basic timestamp ordering method, and an optimistic method based on global timestamps. The performance of the methods are ordered as: two-phase locking, optimistic two-phase locking (described below), distributed optimistic concurrency control, which in most cases outperforms the basic timestamp ordering and the wound-wait methods, which have a similar performance. Also optimistic two-phase locking is best suited for a fully replicated database.

A simulation study of the distributed WDL method is reported in [FHRT92], where it is shown to outperform the standard locking and the wound-wait methods. More interestingly a number of alternative distributed WDL methods are proposed for improved performance.

6.3 Data Sharing or Shared Disk Systems

A method to exceed the performance limitation of a single computer (e.g., a multiprocessor) is to provide multiple computers connectivity to the disk sub-system on which the database resides and a software layer to coordinate their activity [Rahm93b]. In addition to concurrency control, *coherency control* is necessary because of the main memory caching of database pages, which on the one hand reduces the frequency of disk I/Os, but results in *buffer invalidation* when a page updated by one system also resides in the database buffer of the other systems. A similar situation is true for *client/server systems* and *distributed shared memory systems*.

Primary copy locking, where each node is responsible for a database partition, is preferable to a *central lock manager,* because [Rahm93b]: (i) the proper use of primary copy locking ensues in a load balancing effect; (ii) *affinity based routing* to match incoming transactions to the database partitions at each node reduces inter-node communication. A hardware synchronization mechanism, which is treated as an I/O device can be used to detect lock conflicts [Robi85]. The determination of whether an object is locked or not takes a very short time (of the order of few microseconds) and hence the lock request is treated as a synchronous I/O operation (no context switching is required). The *sole interest approach* is an optimization applied to centralized lock manager method, where a node is designated to hold locks on certain objects, but this designation can be varied.

Broadcast invalidation may be used for coherency control, such that as part of transaction commit other nodes holding copies of updated pages are asked to purge their buffers. Lock management can be combined with checking the validity of the page available at a node, which is referred to as *on-request invalidation* or *check-on-access*. Concurrency control and coherency control can be integrated, such that a lock request contains the version number of the requested page on that system. In addition to the granting of the lock, the newest version of the page is sent to the requesting node (if it differs from the node's version). Reciprocally, when a lock is released at a node other than the primary node for the data page, the release of an exclusive lock with the No-Force commit method is accompanied with the transmission of the modified page to its primary node. Improved methods for integrated concurrency and coherency control with fine granularity locking appear in [MoNa91], which also reviews earlier work in Section 4. Adaptive locking strategies for data sharing environments, which "adapt to the contention among users by adjusting the number of locks required, as well as the number of lock requests per transaction", are described in [Josh91].

Trace-driven simulation studies of data-sharing systems are reported in [Rahm93b], while analytic models emphasizing the effect of coherency control appear in [DanA91].

A global extended memory can be provided for system-wide concurrency and coherency control in data sharing systems, and to improve I/O performance. A simulation study to evaluate the performance of such a system is reported in [Rahm93a].

6.4 Multidatabase Transaction Management

Consider a distributed database consisting of heterogeneous databases with different concurrency control and transaction recovery methods. Local transactions are run under the control of a local DBMS, while a multidatabase system is provided to run global transactions. The multidatabase system is to accomplish its task with minimal modifications to system operation [BGMS92]. As noted in [BGMS92] most research to date has been concerned on how to run transactions in a heterogeneous environment, without attention being paid to performance issues: "For example, how much more expensive will it be to run transactions when each box runs a different concurrency control protocol?" Chapter 5 in [RaCh96] is also concerned with multidatabases.

CHAPTER 7: CONCLUSIONS

We have surveyed major recent developments in concurrency control methods, with the emphasis on high-performance, high-contention transaction
processing environments, and provided a self-complete description of locking,
optimistic, and hybrid methods, which combine locking and optimistic methods. We summarized conclusions of previous simulation and analytic results
regarding the performance characteristics of concurrency control methods,
with emphasis on their relative performance. Analytical solution methods for
evaluating the performance of standard locking, restart-oriented locking
methods, and optimistic concurrency control methods were also outlined.

The key insights derived from analytic and simulation studies is summarized at this point.

1. The single metric α uniquely determines the lock contention level in an
   idealized standard locking system with identical per step processing times.
   The system thrashes beyond the critical value $\alpha^* = 0.226$, which is just beyond the point where the maximum throughput in a system with infinite
   resources is attained. The number of active transactions and hence the
   throughput is maximized at the point where the fraction of blocked transactions is at $\beta \simeq 0.3$, which holds for various transaction size distributions
   considered in [Thom93b].

   In a system with finite resources, the maximum throughput is determined
   by the bottleneck resource (at an MPL where the bottleneck resource is
   saturated). This usually occurs well before the MPL at which the mean
   number of active transactions is maximized.

2. Factors contributing to the thrashing behavior of standard locking are as
   follows: (i) sudden increases in the number of activated transactions; (ii)
   an undesirable composition of activated transactions, e.g., long transactions, although a maximum MPL limit is in effect; (iii) temporary increase
   in the number of accesses to hot-spots.

3. The mean number of locks held per transaction depends on the second
   moment of requested locks (see equation (3.8)), hence the probability of
   lock conflict increases with the variability of transaction size. For transactions of size k the probability of lock conflict (resp. the probability of
   deadlock per transaction, P_D) is proportional to k^2 (resp. k^4) [GrRe92].
   Furthermore, P_D depends on the third moment of transaction size, which
   for a fixed mean transaction size may have a major effect on increasing
   P_D [ThRy91].

4. The mean waiting time incurred by a transaction which requests a lock
   held by an active transaction (W_1) is one third of the mean residence time
   of the active transaction, which requests its locks uniformly over its resi-

dence time. The mean overall waiting time (W) depends on the probability of being blocked at a certain level i and the associated waiting time. It follows from equation (3.10) which holds in a system with variable size transactions with identical transaction steps that at the point where the number of active transactions is maximized ($\beta \simeq 0.3$) we have $W \simeq 1.4 W_1$. The system tends to thrash beyond this point and is hence of little interest.

In the case of variable size transactions with identical transaction steps W_1 is proportional to the third moment of the number of requested locks, which is related to the skewness of the distribution.

5. When the per step processing times with standard locking are different, another metric ρ, which is the fraction of lock conflicts with blocked transactions, is a more appropriate measure of lock contention. As the duration of the last transaction step, which has the most effect on lock contention is varied, simulation results show that ρ varies in the range $0.2 \leq \rho \leq 0.3$. This is consistent with the conflict ratio metric which is equal to $(1 - \rho)^{-1}$, obtained from trace-driven studies in [MoWe92]. Since β is an easy to measure parameter and transaction throughput is maximized at $\beta \simeq 0.3$, it follows that it is an appropriate performance metric for load control for the homogeneous database access model in a lock contention bound system.

6. In the case of the "more realistic lock contention model" in [Thom94a], ρ was observed to vary over a wider range in a set of semi-randomly selected configurations. Experimental results in [WHMZ94] seem to indicate that the conflict ratio varies in a rather narrow range, which makes both metrics useful for load control purposes.

7. Restart-oriented locking methods reduce the level of lock contention at the cost of additional processing. In a lock contention bound system significant increases in the maximum throughput attainable by the system are possible. The WDL [FrRT92] and the modified WDL [Thom92] methods outperform the asymmetric running priority method, because they ensue in less wasted processing than the symmetric running priority method. This is accomplished through heuristics which take into account transaction progress.

The asymmetric running priority method can outperform both the WDL and the modified WDL methods in a system with limited hardware resources, because it results in less wasted processing than both methods.

8. Optimistic concurrency control methods are susceptible to abort according to a quadratic effect, i.e., the probability of an unsuccessful validation increases as the square of transaction size [FrRT92]. Numerical results based on the performance analysis in [RyTh87] show that in a system with variable transaction sizes most of the wasted processing is due to the largest transactions. This analysis shows that the wasted processing due to the optimistic kill method is one-half of the optimistic die method.

9. Two-phase transaction processing methods reduce the effective level of transaction concurrency to attain higher transaction throughputs. Thus even if the first execution phase of a transaction is unsuccessful, it has the beneficial effect of prefetching the data from disk, which can be used by the second execution phase provided access invariance prevails.

There has been little effort in utilizing the analysis of locking methods to performance evaluation of transaction processing systems, which is due to the difficulty of characterizing transaction processing systems from the lock contention viewpoint. An important consideration in this respect is the validation of the results provided by the analysis against measurement results rather than just simulations. There are several areas for further investigation, which can be summarized as follows:

1. *Measurement of lock contention levels* are provided by most DBMSs (see e.g., [CLSW84],[IBMC95]). Unfortunately, this information is not sufficiently detailed and cannot be easily correlated with other events in the system.

   This is reminiscent of the performance evaluation of multiprogrammed computer systems two decades ago. In spite of the availability of analytical models, performance prediction studies were not possible until better instrumentation and data reduction packages became available [LZGS84].

2. *Workload characterization* is very important for building more realistic models. Unfortunately some recent efforts have been handicapped due to the proprietary nature of database contents, i.e., researchers have been provided with lock traces with little information about the database and other aspects of the system, such as transaction scheduling, which affects the lock contention level (see e.g., [SiSm94]).

3. Given the complexity of database workloads, trace-driven simulation of concurrency control methods is a viable alternative (see e.g., [Rahm93b]). There are however several limitations, in that, for example, it is usually difficult to modify the traces to study the effect of an increased transaction arrival rate.

4. Given the very detailed nature of simulations required for evaluating the performance of concurrency control methods, especially taking into account recovery overhead, prototyping is a viable alternative to simulation. Unfortunately, aspects leading to an industrial strength implementation are usually omitted from prototypes.

Some additional topics related to concurrency control are as follows.

Concurrency control and recovery issues in "advanced database applications" or "unconventional transaction management" [BaKa91],[Elma92], [RaCh96], and transactions for workflow systems [LeAl94] are areas requiring further investigation. Some of the associated problems have to do more with scheduling and coordinating related activities, rather than concurrency control. Some aspects of advanced and cooperating transactions have been addressed in Section 3.6 in Chapter 3.

Special locking requirements for *temporal databases* is another area requiring further investigation [TCG+92].

Real-time transaction processing or *real-time databases* is another area affected by concurrency control. In systems with *soft deadlines*, the performance measure of interest is *transaction timeliness*, which is the value rendered to the system as specified by a decreasing function of transaction's completion time, past transaction's deadline, say $f(t_{comp.} - t_{deadline})$. When $t_{comp.} \geq t_{deadline}$ for firm deadlines $f(t_{comp.} - t_{deadline}) = 0$ and for *hard deadlines* $f(t_{comp.} - t_{deadline}) = -\infty$, i.e., missing the deadline results in a catastrophe. Various concurrency control methods have been evaluated to determine their suitability for real-time transaction processing and many new concurrency control methods have been proposed for this purpose [Rama93],[RaCh96]. These include a method based on access invariance, because it provides an opportunity to preanalyze the objects required by the transaction for its second execution phase [ONRP95] and the hybrid optimistic concurrency control method (HSRT91). Transaction spawning for improving performance in real-time systems has been considered in [BeBr95]. The performance of firm real-time concurrency control methods are described and compared in [HaCL95].

Active databases [Chak95] are intended to provide timely responses to time-critical events and this is accomplished by providing *event-condition-action rules* to be specified for the DBMS [Daya95]. In the case of an inventory control application, the *event* may be the update of an item's QOH, the *condition* QOH + Q_on_order < Threshold and the *action* reorder the item if the above condition is true. A performance evaluation of active DBMSs which takes into account locking effects and distinguishes between external and rule management tasks is reported in [CaJL91]. Different degrees of coupling among these two types of tasks are considered and their effect on system performance evaluated.

Numerous additional suggestions for further research appear throughout the text.

APPENDIX: NOTATION FOR IMPORTANT PARAMETERS

A Ratio of mean transaction blocking time with a single level of blocking and mean transaction response time ($A = W_1/R(M)$).

α Mean number of lock conflicts per transaction times the normalized waiting time for single level blocking ($\alpha = K_1 P_c A$ with $A = W_1/R(M)$).

β Fraction of transactions which are in the blocked state ($\beta = K_1 P_c W/R(M) = \overline{M}_b/M = 1 - \overline{M}_a/M$).

C_k Transactions in class $1 \leq k \leq K$.

D The number of data items and associated locks in the database.

f_k Fraction of transactions introduced into the system which are in C_k, $1 \leq k \leq K$; $\sum_{k=1}^{K} f_k = 1$.

K Number of transaction classes.

K_i The ith moment of the number of requested locks by transactions.

$\overline{L}$ The mean number of locks held per transaction.

$\overline{L}_a(\overline{L}_b)$ The mean number of locks held by a transaction while it is active (blocked) ($\overline{L} = \overline{L}_a + \overline{L}_b$).

$\overline{L}_k$ The mean number of locks held by transactions in C_k.

M The number of transactions in the closed system.

$\overline{M}_k$ Mean number of transactions in C_k, such that $M = \sum_{k=1}^{K} \overline{M}_k$.

$\overline{M}_a(\overline{M}_b)$ The mean number of active (blocked) transactions in the system ($\overline{M}_a = (1 - \beta)M$ and $\overline{M}_b = \beta M$).

$\hat{M}$ The multiprogramming level which maximizes the number of active transactions in the system ($\overline{M}_a$) and potentially system throughput.

v Inverse of mean level of lock contention per transaction ($1/v = K_1\overline{L}A/N = \alpha/(M - 1) \simeq \alpha/M$).

P_c Probability of lock conflict per lock request.

$P_b(i)$ Probability distribution of the effective level of transaction blocking ($P_b(i) = \rho^{i-1}, i > 1, P_b(1) = 1 - \rho/(1 - \rho)$).

$r_k(M)$ The mean response time for transactions in C_k as determined by hardware resource contention only.

$r(M)$ The mean response time over all transaction classes as determined by hardware resource contention only $r(M) = \sum_{k=1}^{K} r_k(M)f_k$.

$R_k(M)$ The mean response time for transactions in C_k ($R_k(M) = (k+1)s(\overline{M}_a) + kP_cW$).

$R(M)$ The mean response time over all transaction classes ($R(M) = \sum_{k=1}^{K} R_k(M)f_k$ and $R(M) = r(\overline{M}_a)/(1-\beta)$).

ρ Fraction of lock conflicts which are with a blocked transaction (in a system with identically distributed processing times for transaction steps $\rho \simeq \beta$).

$s(\overline{M}_a)$ The mean processing time of a transaction step with $\overline{M}_a$ active transactions in the system.

$s'(\overline{M}_a)$ The mean residual processing time of a transaction step.

$t(M)$ System throughput as determined by hardware resource contention with M transactions and no lock contention. $t(M)$, $M \geq 1$ is referred to as the system throughput characteristic.

$T(M)$ Transaction throughput with M transactions in the system as affected by hardware resource and lock contention. $T(M)$, $M \geq 1$ is referred to as the effective throughput characteristic.

W_1 The mean transaction waiting time due to a lock conflict with an active transaction.

W The mean overall transaction waiting time due to a lock conflict.

REFERENCES

[ACMc87] R. Agrawal, M. J. Carey, and L. W. McVoy. "The performance of alternative strategies for dealing with deadlocks in database management systems," *IEEE Transactions on Software Engineering 13*,12 (December 1987), 1348-1363.

[AEAL94] D. Agrawal, A. El Abbadi, and A. E. Lang. "The performance of protocols based on locks with ordered sharing," *IEEE Transactions on Knowledge and Data Engineering 6*,5 (October 1994), 805-818.

[AgCL87] R. Agrawal, M. J. Carey, and M. Livny. "Concurrency control performance modeling: Alternatives and implications," *ACM Transactions on Database Systems 12*,4 (December 1987), 609-654.

[BaGM92] D. Barbara and H. Garcia-Molina. "The demarcation protocol: A technique for maintaining arithmetic constraints in distributed database systems," *Proceedings of the International Conference on Extending Database Technology EDBT-92*, Springer-Verlag, 1992, pp. 371-397.

[BaKa91] N. S. Barghouti and G. E. Kaiser. "Concurrency control in advanced database applications," *ACM Computing Surveys 23*,3 (September 1991), 269-317.

[BaRa92] B. R. Badrinath and K. Ramamithram. "Semantics-based concurrency control: Beyond commutativity," *ACM Transactions on Database Systems 17*,1 (March 1992), 163-199.

[Baye86] R. Bayer. "Consistency of transactions and random batch," *ACM Transactions on Database Systems 11*,4 (December 1986), 397-404.

[BCFP87] C. Boksenbaum, M. Cart, J. Ferrie', and J. F. Pons. "Concurrent certification by interval of timestamps in distributed database systems," *IEEE Transactions on Software Engineering 13*,4 (April 1987), 409-419.

[BDH+84] A. Blum, L. Donatiello, P. Heidelberger, S. S. Lavenberg, and E. MacNair. "Experiments with decomposition of extended queueing network models," in *Modeling Techniques and Tools for Performance Analysis*, D. Potier (Editor), North-Holland, 1984, pp. 623-640.

[BeBr95] A. Bestavros and S. Braoudakis "Value-cognizant speculative concurrency control," *Proc. 21st Conf. Very Large Data Bases*, Zurich, Switzerland, Sept. 1995, Morgan Kauffman, pp. 122-133.

[BeGo81] P. A. Bernstein and N. Goodman. "Concurrency control in distributed database systems," *ACM Computing Surveys 13*,2 (June 1981), 185-221.

[BeHG87] P. A. Bernstein, V. Hadzilacos, and N. Goodman. *Concurrency Control and Recovery in Database Systems*, Addison-Wesley, 1987.

[BGMS92] Y. Breitbart, H. Garcia-Molina, and A. Silberschatz. "Overview of multidatabase transaction management," *Very Large Data Base Journal 2*, (1992), 181-239.

[BlBu93] M. L. Blount and M. Butrico. "DSVM6L: Distributed virtual shared memory on a RISC System/6000," *Proceedings 1993 IEEE COMPCON*, San Francisco, CA, February 1993, pp. 491-499.

[BoCa92] P. M. Bober and M. J. Carey. "On mixing queries and trans- actions via multiversion locking," *Proceedings 8th International Conference on Data Engineering*, Tempe, AZ, February 1992, IEEE Computer Society Press, pp. 535-545.

[BrMc84] A. Brandwajn and B. McCormack. "Efficient approximation for models of multiprogramming with shared domains," *Proceedings 1984 ACM SIGMETRICS Conference on Measurement and Mod- eling of Computer Systems*, Boston, MA, August 1984, pp. 186-194.

[BuTh94] A. Burger and P. Thanisch. "Branching transactions: A trans- action model for parallel database systems," *Directions in Data- bases: Proceedings 12th National Conference on Databases, BNCOD 12*, D. S. Bowers (Editor), Guildford, UK, July 1994, pp. 121-136.

[CaJL91] M. J. Carey, R. Jauhari, and M. Livny. "On transaction bounda- ries in active databases: A performance perspective," *IEEE Transactions on Knowledge and Data Engineering 3,3* (Sept. 1991), 320-336.

[CaLi89] M. J. Carey and M. Livny. "Parallelism and concurrency control performance in distributed database machines," *Proceedings 1989 ACM SIGMOD International Conference on Management of Data*, Portland, OR, June 1989, pp. 122-133.

[CaLi91] M. J. Carey and M. Livny. "Conflict detection tradeoffs for repli- cated data," *ACM Transactions on Database Systems 16,4* (De- cember 1991), 703-746.

[Casa81] M. A. Casanova. *The Concurrency Control Problem for Database Systems, Lecture Notes in Computer Science 116*, Springer- Verlag, 1981.

[CeGM88] W. Cellary, E. Gelenbe, and T. Morzy. *Concurrency Control in Distributed Databases*, North-Holland, 1988.

[CePe84] S. Ceri and G. Pelagatti. *Distributed Databases-Principles and Systems*, McGraw-Hill, 1984.

[Chak95]   S. Chakravarthy. "Early active database efforts: A capsule sum-
              mary," *IEEE Transactions on Knowledge and Data Engineering*
              7,6 (December 1995), 1008-1010.

[ChGM83]   A. Chesnais, E. Gelenbe, and I. Mitrani. "On the modeling of
              parallel access to shared data," *Communications of the ACM*
              26,3 (March 1983), 198-202.

[CHKS91]   S. Ceri, M. A. W. Houtsma, A. M. Keller, and P. Samarati. "A
              classification of update methods for replicated databases," *Tech-
              nical Report STAN-CS-91-1932*, Stanford University, October 1991.

[ChNe82]   K. M. Chandy and D. Neuse. "Linearizer: A heuristic algorithm
              for queueing network models of computer systems, *Communi-
              cations of the ACM 25*,2 (February 1982), 126-134.

[Chri84]   S. Christodoulakis. "Implications of certain assumptions in data-
              base performance evaluation," *ACM Transactions on Database
              Systems 9*,2 (June 1984), 163-186.

[CLSW84]   J. M. Cheng, C. R. Loosley, A. Shibamiya, and P. S. Worthington.
              "IBM Database 2 performance: Design, implementation, and tun-
              ing," *IBM Systems Journal 23*,2 (1984), 189-210.

[Cour77]   P. J. Courtois. *Decomposability: Queueing and Computer System
              Applications*, Academic Press, 1977.

[DanA91]   A. Dan. *Performance Analysis of Data Sharing Environments*, The
              MIT Press, 1991.

[Date83]   C. J. Date. *An Introduction to Database Systems, Vol. II*,
              Addison-Wesley, 1983.

[Daya95]   U. Dayal. "Ten years of activity in active database systems: What
              have we accomplished," *Active and Real-Time Database Systems
              -ARTDB-95*, M. Berndtsson and J. Hansson (Eds.), Springer-
              Verlag, 1995, pp. 3-22.

[EGLT76]   K. P. Eswaran, J. N. Gray, R. A. Lorie, and I. L. Traiger. "The
              notions of consistency and predicate locks in a database system,"
              Communications of the ACM 19,11 (November 1976), 624-633.

[Elma92]   A. K. Elmagarmid (Editor). *Database Transaction Models for Ad-
              vanced Applications*, Morgan Kauffman, 1992.

[FeSZ83]   D. Ferrari, G. Serrazi, and A. Zeigner. *Measurement and Tuning
              of Computer Systems*, Prentice-Hall, 1983.

[FHRT93]   P. A. Franaszek, J. R. Haritsa, J. T. Robinson, and A. Thomasian.
              "Distributed concurrency control based on limited wait depth,"
              IEEE Transactions on Parallel and Distributed Systems 4,11 (No-
              vember 1993), 1246-1264.

[FrRo85]   P. Franaszek and J. T. Robinson. "Limitations of concurrency in transaction processing," *ACM Transactions on Database Systems* *10*,1 (March 1985), 1-28.

[FrRT90]   P. Franaszek, J. T. Robinson, and A. Thomasian. "Access invariance and its use in high contention environments," *Proceedings 6th International Conference on Data Engineering,* Los Angeles, CA, February 1990, IEEE Computer Society Press, pp. 47-55.

[FrRT91a]   P. A. Franaszek, J. T. Robinson, and A. Thomasian. "Adaptive concurrency control scheme for transaction processing," *IBM Technical Disclosure Bulletin 33*,9 (February 1991), 29-30.

[FrRT91b]   P. A. Franaszek, J. T. Robinson, and A. Thomasian. "Integrated concurrency control/CPU scheduling," *IBM Technical Disclosure Bulletin 33*,9 (February 1991), 37-40.

[FrRT92]   P. Franaszek, J. T. Robinson, and A. Thomasian. "Concurrency control for high contention environments," *ACM Transactions on Database Systems 17*,2 (June 1992), 304-345.

[Full68]   W. Fuller. *An Introduction to Probability Theory and Its Applications, Volume I, 3rd Edition,* John Wiley and Sons, 1968.

[GaBo83]   B. I. Galler and L. Bos. "A model of transaction blocking in databases," *Performance Evaluation 3* (1983), 95-122.

[Gibs91]   G. A. Gibson. *Redundant Disk Arrays,* The MIT Press, 1991.

[GMol83]   H. Garcia-Molina. "Using semantic knowledge for transaction processing in a distributed database," *ACM Transactions on Database Systems 8*,2 (June 1993), 186-213.

[GMSa87]   H. Garcia-Molina and K. Salem. "Sagas," *Proceedings 1987 ACM SIGMOD International Conference on Management of Data,* San Francisco, CA, May 1987, pp. 249-259.

[GMSa92]   H. Garcia-Molina and K. Salem. "Main memory database systems: An overview," *IEEE Transactions on Knowledge and Data Engineering 4*,6 (December 1992), 509-516.

[GoTh92]   L. Golubchik and A. Thomasian. "Token allocation in distributed systems," *Proceedings International Conference on Distributed Computing Systems,* Yokohama, Japan, June 1992, IEEE Computer Society Press, pp. 64-71.

[Gray80]   J. N. Gray. Experience with System R lock manager. IBM San Jose Research Center, Internal Memo, Spring 1980 (see [Date83]).

[Gray88]   J. N. Gray. "The cost of messages," *Proceedings 7th ACM Annual Symposium of Principles of Distributed Computing,* Toronto, Ontario, Canada, August 1988, pp. 1-7.

[Gray93] J. N. Gray (Editor), *The Benchmark Handbook for Transaction Processing Systems, 2nd Edition,* Morgan Kauffman, 1993.

[GrRe92] J. N. Gray and A. Reuter. *Transaction Processing: Concepts and Facilities,* Morgan Kauffman, 1992.

[HaCL95] J. R. Haritsa, M. C. Carey, and M. Livny. "Firm real-time concurrency control," Chapter 17 in *Performance of Concurrency Control Mechanisms in Centralized Database Systems,* V. Kumar (Editor), Prentice-Hall, 1995, pp. 461–493.

[Haer84] T. Haerder. "Observations on optimistic concurrency control schemes," *Information Systems 9,2* (1984), 111-120.

[HaRo93] T. Haerder and K. Rothermel. "Concurrency control issues in nested transactions," *Very Large Data Base Journal 2* (1993), 39-74.

[Herl90] M. Herlihy. "Apologizing versus asking permission: Optimistic concurrency control methods for abstract data types," *ACM Transactions on Database Systems 15,1* (March 1990), 96-124.

[HsLa88] MC-T. Hsieh and S. S. Lam. "PAM - A noniterative approximate solution method for closed multichain queueing networks," *Performance Evaluation 9* (1988-89), 119-133.

[HSRT91] J. Huang, J. A. Stankovic. K. Ramamithram, and D. Towsley. "Experimental evaluation of real-time optimistic concurrency control schemes," *Proceedings 17th International Conference on Very Large Databases,* September 1991, Barcelona, Spain, Morgan Kauffman, pp. 35-46.

[HsZh92] M. Hsu and B. Zhang. "Performance evaluation of cautious waiting," *ACM Transactions on Database Systems 17,3* (September 1992), 477-512.

[HsZh95] M. Hsu and B. Zhang. "Modeling performance impact of hot spots," Chapter 7 in *Performance of Concurrency Control Mechanisms in Centralized Database Systems,* V. Kumar (Editor), Prentice-Hall, 1995, pp. 148-164.

[IBMC94] IBM Corp. *IMS/ESA Version 4, System Administration Guide,* SC26-3975, July 1994.

[IBMC95] IBM Corp. *DB2 for MVS/ESA, Version 4, Administration Guide, Volumes 1 and 2* SC26-3265, November 1995.

[ImBa94] T. Imielinski and B. R. Badrinath. "Moble wireless computing," *Communications of the ACM 37,10* (October 1994), 18-28.

[IrLi79] K. B. Irani and H. L. Lin. "Queueing network models for concurrent transaction processing in database systems," *Proceedings 1979 ACM International SIGMOD Conference on Management of Data,* Boston, MA, June 1979, pp. 134-142.

[JaSh92]   H. V. Jagadish and O. Shmuelli. "A proclamation based model for cooperating transactions," *Proceedings 18th Conference on Very Large Data Bases,* Vancouver, Canada, August 1992, Morgan Kauffman, pp. 265-276.

[JeKT88]   B. C. Jenq, W. H. Kohler, and D. Towsley. "A queueing network model for a distributed database testbed," *IEEE Transactions on Software Engineering 14,*7 (July 1988), 908-921.

[JeTK89]   B. C. Jenq, B. C. Twichell, and T. W. Keller. "Locking performance in a shared nothing parallel database machine," *IEEE Transactions on Knowledge and Data Engineering 1,*4 (December 1989), 530-543.

[JoKo77]   N. L. Johnson and S. Kotz. *Urn Models and Their Application,* Wiley, 1977.

[Josh91]   A. M. Joshi. "Adaptive locking strategies in a multi-node data sharing environment," *Proceedings 17th International Conference on Very Large Databases,* Barcelona, Spain, September 1991, Morgan Kauffman, pp. 181-191.

[JoSh93]   T. Johnson and D. Shasha. "The performance of concurrent B-tree algorithms," *ACM Transactions on Database Systems 18,*1 (March 1993), 51-101.

[KeTe84]   M. L. Kersten and H. Tebra. "Application of an optimistic concurrency control method," *Software - Practice and Experience 14,*2 (1984), 153-168.

[Klei75]   L. Kleinrock. *Queueing Systems, Volume I: Theory,* John Wiley and Sons, 1975.

[Knap87]   E. Knapp. "Deadlock detection in distributed databases," *ACM Computing Surveys 1,*4 (December 1987), 303-328.

[Koba81]   H. Kobayashi. *Modeling and Analysis: System Performance Evaluation Methodology,* Addison-Wesley, Reading, MA, 1981.

[Kort83]   H. F. Korth. "Locking primitives in a database system," *Journal of the ACM 30,*1 (January 1983), 55-79.

[KrBe94]   N. Krishnakumar and A. J. Bernstein. "Bounded ignorance: A technique for increasing concurrency in a replicated system," *ACM Transactions on Database Systems 19,*4 (December 1994), 586-625.

[Kuma90]   A. Kumar. "An analysis of borrowing policies for escrow transactions in a replicated data environment," *Proceedings 6th International Conference on Data Engineering,* Los Angeles, CA, February 1990, IEEE Computer Society Press, pp. 446-454.

[Kuma95]   V. Kumar (Editor). *Performance of Concurrency Control Mechanisms in Centralized Database Systems,* Prentice-Hall, 1995.

[KuRo81]   H. T. Kung and J. T. Robinson. "On optimistic concurrency control methods," *ACM Transactions on Database Systems 6,2* (June 1981), 213-226.

[KuSt92]   A. Kumar and M. Stonebraker. "Semantics based transaction management techniques for replicated data," *Proceedings 1992 ACM SIGMOD International Conference on Management of Data*, San Diego, CA, June 1992, pp. 175-186.

[LaSh82]   A. M. Langer and A. W. Shum. "The distribution of granule accesses made by database transactions," *Communications of the ACM 25*, 11 (November 1982), 831-832.

[Lave83]   S. S. Lavenberg (Editor). *Computer Performance Modeling Handbook*, Academic Press, 1983.

[Lave84]   S. S. Lavenberg. "A simple analysis of exclusive and shared lock contention   a   database   system," *Proceedings 1984 ACM SIGMETRICS Conference on Measurement and Modeling of Computer Systems*, Boston, MA, August 1984, pp. 143-148.

[LeAl94]   F. Leymann and W. Altenhuber. "Managing business processes as an information resource," *IBM Systems Journal 33,2* (1994), 326-348.

[LeRo85]   M. D. P. Leland and W. D. Roome. "The Silicon database machine," *Proceedings 4th International Workshop on Database Machines*, Grand Bahamas Island, March 1985, Springer-Verlag, pp. 169-189.

[LiNa88]   K. Li and J. F. Naughton. "Multiprocessor main memory transaction processing," *Proceedings International Symposium on Databases in Parallel and Distributed Systems*, Austin, TX, December 1988, IEEE Computer Society Press, pp. 177-187.

[LiNo82]   W. K. Lin and J. Nolte. "Performance of two-phase locking," *Proceedings 6th Berkeley Workshop on Distributed Data Management and Computer Networks*, Berkeley, CA, February 1982, pp. 131-160.

[LMWF94]   N. Lynch, M. Merritt, W. Weihl, and A. Fekete. *Atomic Transactions*, Morgan Kauffman, 1994.

[LZGS84]   E. D. Lazowska, J. Zahorjan, G. S. Graham, and K. C. Sevcik. *Quantitative System Performance: Computer System Analysis Using Queueing Network Models*, Prentice-Hall, 1984.

[MaCB84]   M. A. Marsan, G. Conte, and G. Balbo. "A class of generalized stochastic Petri nets for the performance evaluation of multiprocessor systems," *ACM Transactions on Computer Systems (TOCS) 2,2* (May 1984), 93-122.

[Mass86]   W. Massey. "A probabilistic analysis of database system," *Proceedings Joint Performance 86 and 1986 ACM SIGMETRICS*

Conference on Measurement and Modeling of Computer Systems, Raleigh, NC, May 1986, pp. 141-146.

[MeNa82] D. A. Menasce and T. Nakanishi. "Optimistic versus pessimistic concurrency control mechanisms in database managements systems," *Information Systems 7*,1 (1982), 13-27.

[MHL+92] C. Mohan, D. Haderle, B. Lindsay, H. Pirahesh, and P. Schwartz. "ARIES: A transaction recovery method supporting fine granularity locking and partial rollbacks using write-ahead locking," *ACM Transactions on Database Systems 17*,1 (March 1992), 94-162.

[Mitr85] D. Mitra. "Probabilistic models and asymptotic results for concurrent processing with exclusive and non-exclusive locks," *SIAM Journal Computing 14*,4 (November 1985), 1030-1051.

[Moha90] C. Mohan. "Commit_LSN: A novel and simple method for reducing locking and latching in transaction processing systems," *Proceedings 16th International Conference on Very Large Data bases,* Brisbane, Australia, August 1990, Morgan Kauffman, pp. 406-418.

[Moha92a] C. Mohan. "Interaction between query optimization and concurrency control," *Proceedings 2nd International Workshop on Research Issues on Data Engineering,* Tempe, AZ, February 1992, IEEE Computer Society Press, pp. 26-35.

[Moha92b] C. Mohan. "Less optimism about optimistic concurrency control," *Proceedings 2nd International Workshop on Research Issues on Data Engineering,* Tempe, AZ, February 1992, IEEE Computer Society Press, pp. 199-204.

[Moha95] C. Mohan. "Concurrency control and recovery methods for B+ tree indexes: ARIES/KVL and ARIES/IM," Chapter 10 in *Performance of Concurrency Control Mechanisms in Centralized Database Systems,* V. Kumar (Editor), Prentice-Hall, 1995, pp. 248-306.

[MoLe92] C. Mohan and F. Levine. "ARIES/IM: An efficient and high concurrency index management method using write-ahead logging," *Proceedings 1992 ACM SIGMOD International Conference on Management of Data,* San Diego, CA, June 1992, pp. 371-380.

[MoNa91] C. Mohan and I. Narang. "Recovery and coherency control protocols for fast intersystem page transfer and fine granularity locking in a shared disks transaction management," *Proceedings 17th International Conference on Very Large Databases,* Barcelona, Spain, September 1991, Morgan Kauffman, pp. 193-207.

[Mont78] W. A. Montgomery. "Robust concurrency control for a distributed information system," *MIT-LCS-TR-207,* MIT, Laboratory for Computer Science, Cambridge, MA, December 1978.

[MoPL92]   C. Mohan, H. Pirahesh, and R. Lorie. "Efficient and flexible methods for transient versioning of records to avoid locking by read-only transactions," *Proceedings 1992 ACM International SIGMOD Conference on Management of Data,* San Diego, CA, June 1992, pp. 124-133.

[Moss85]   J. E. B. Moss. *Nested Transactions: An Approach to Reliable Distributed Computing,* MIT Press, 1985.

[MoWe92]   A. Moenkeberg and G. Weikum. "Performance evaluation of an adaptive and robust load control method for the avoidance of data contention thrashing," *Proceedings 18th International Conference on Very Large Data Bases,* Vancouver, Canada, August 1992, Morgan Kauffman, pp. 432-443.

[MoWo84]   R. J. T. Morris and W. S. Wong. "Performance of concurrency control algorithms with non-exclusive accesses," *Performance '84: Proceedings 10th International Symposium on Computer Performance,* E. Gelenbe (Editor), Paris, France, December 1984, North Holland, pp. 87-101.

[MoWo85]   R. J. T. Morris and W. S. Wong. "Performance analysis of locking and optimistic concurrency control algorithms," *Performance Evaluation 5,2* (1985), 105-118.

[MuTa85]   S. J. Mullender and A. S. Tanenbaum. "A distributed file service based on optimistic concurrency control," *Proceedings 10th ACM Symposium on Operating System Principles,* Orcas Island, WA, December 1985, pp. 51-62.

[NaMe84]   T. Nakanishi and D. M. Menasce. "Correctness and performance evaluation of two-phase commit-based protocol for DDBs," *Computer Performance 5,*1 (March 1984), IPC Press, UK, 38-54.

[Ober80]   R. Obermarck. "IMS/VS program isolation feature," *IBM Research Report RJ 2879,* San Jose, CA, July 1980.

[ONei86]   P. E. O'Neil. "The escrow transaction method," *ACM Transactions on Database Systems 11,*4 (December 1986), 405-430.

[ONRP95]   P. E. O'Neil, K. Ramamithram, and C. Pu. "A two-phase approach to predictably scheduling real-time transactions," Chapter 18 in *Performance of Concurrency Control Mechanisms in Centralized Database Systems,* V. Kumar (Editor), Prentice-Hall, 1995, pp. 494-592.

[Ozsu94]   M. T. Ozsu. "Transaction models and transaction management in object-oriented database management systems," in *Advances in Object-Oriented Data base Systems,* A. Dogac, M. T. Ozsu, A. Biliris, and T. Sellis (Editors), Springer-Verlag, 1994, pp. 147-184.

[Papa86]   C. Papadimitiou. *The Theory of Database Concurrency Control,* Computer Science Press, 1986.

[PeRS88]　P. Peinl, A. Reuter, and H. Sammer. "High contention in a stock trading database: A case study," *Proceedings 1988 ACM SIGMOD International Conference on Management of Data,* Chicago, IL, June 1988, pp. 260-268.

[PoLe80]　D. Potier and Ph. LeBlanc. "Analysis of locking policies in database management systems," *Communications of the ACM 23,*10 (October 1980), 584-593.

[PrSU86]　U. Pradel, G. Schlageter, and R. Unland. "Redesign of optimistic methods: Improving performance and applicability," *Proceedings 2nd International Conference on Data Engineering,* Los Angeles, CA, February 1986, IEEE Computer Society Press, pp. 466-473.

[PuLe91]　C. Pu and A. Leff. "Replica control in in distributed databases: An asynchronous approach," *Proceedings 1991 ACM SIGMOD International Conference on Management of Data,* Denver, CO, May 1991, pp. 377-386.

[RaCh96]　K. Ramamithram and P. K. Chrisanthis. *Advances in Concurrency Control and Transaction Processing,* IEEE Computer Society Press, 1996.

[Rahm93a]　E. Rahm. "Evaluation of closely coupled systems for high performance database processing," *Proceedings 13th International Conference on Distributed Computing Systems,* Pittsburgh, PA, May 1993, pp. 301-310.

[Rahm93b]　E. Rahm. "Empirical performance evaluation of concurrency and coherency control protocols for database sharing systems," *ACM Transactions on Database Systems 18,*2 (June 1993), 333-377.

[Rajk91]　R. Rajkumar. *Synchronization in Real-Time Systems: A Priority Inheritance Approach,* Kluwer Academic Publishers, 1991.

[Rama93]　K. Ramamithram. "Real-time databases," *Distributed and Parallel Databases 1* (1993), 199-226.

[Reut85]　A. Reuter. "The transaction pipeline processor," *International Workshop on High Performance Transaction Systems,* Pacific Grove, CA, September 1985 (presentation and attendees proceedings).

[Reut95]　A. Reuter. "An analytical model of transaction interference," Chapter 4 in *Performance of Concurrency Control Mechanisms in Centralized Database Systems,* V. Kumar (Editor), Prentice-Hall, 1995, pp. 37-57.

[RMRR92]　A. Raghuram, R. W. Morgan, B. Rajaraman, and Y. Ronen. "Approximation for the mean value performance of locking algorithms for distributed database systems: A partitioned database," *Annals of Operations Research 36* (1992), 299-346.

[Robi82]   J. T. Robinson. "Experiments with transaction processing on a multiprocessor," *IBM Research Report RC 9725*, Yorktown Heights, NY, December 1982.

[Robi84]   J. T. Robinson. "Separating policy from correctness in concurrency control design," *Software Practice and Experience 14*,9 (September 1984), 827-844.

[Robi85]   J. T. Robinson. "A fast general-purpose hardware synchronization mechanism," *Proceedings 1985 ACM SIGMOD International Conference on Management of Data*, Austin, TX, May 1985, pp. 122-130.

[Room82]   W. D. Roome. "The intelligent store: A content-addressable page manager," *Bell Systems Technical Journal 61*,9 (1982), 2567-2596.

[RoSL78]   D. J. Rosenkrantz, R. E. Stearns, and P. M. Lewis II. "System level concurrency control for distributed database systems." *ACM Transactions on Database Systems 3*,2 (June 1978), 178-198.

[RyTh87]   I. K. Ryu and A. Thomasian. "Performance evaluation of centralized databases with optimistic concurrency control," *Performance Evaluation 7*,3 (1987), 195-211.

[RyTh88]   I. K. Ryu and A. Thomasian. "Performance analysis of centralized databases with static locking," Unpublished report, IBM T. J. Watson Research Center, Hawthorne, NY, 1988 (available from the second author).

[RyTh90a]   I. K. Ryu and A. Thomasian. "Analysis of database performance with dynamic locking," *Journal of the ACM 37*,3 (July 1990), 491-523.

[RyTh90b]   I. K. Ryu and A. Thomasian. "Performance analysis of dynamic locking with the no-waiting method," *IEEE Transactions on Software Engineering 16*,7 (July 1990), 684-698.

[SBCM95]   G. Samaras, K. Britton, A. Citron, and C. Mohan. "Two-phase commit optimizations in a commercial distributed environment," *Distributed and Parallel Databases*, (1995), 325-360.

[Schw78]   H. D. Schwetman. "Hybrid simulation models of computer systems," *Communications of the ACM 21*,9 (September 1978), 718-723.

[Serr84]   A. E. I. Serry. "An Analytical Approach to Modeling IMS Systems," *Technical Report CSRG-161*, Computer Science Research Group, University of Toronto, Ontario, Canada, July 1984.

[Sevc81]   K. C. Sevcik. "Data base system performance prediction using an analytical model," *Proceedings 7th International Conference on Very Large Data Bases*, Cannes, France, September 1981, ACM Press, pp. 182-198.

[Sevc83]   K. C. Sevcik. "Comparison of concurrency control methods using analytic models," in *Information Processing 83*, R.E.A. Mason (Editor), North-Holland, 1983, pp. 847-858.

[SGMS94]   K. Salem, H. Garcia-Molina, and J. Shands. "Altruistic locking," *ACM Transactions on Database Systems 19*,1 (March 1994), 117-165.

[ShSp81]   A. W. Shum and P. G. Spirakis. "Performance analysis of concurrency control methods in database systems," in *Performance '81*, F. J. Kylstra (Editor), North-Holland, 1981, pp. 1-19.

[Sing91]   M. Singhal. "Performance analysis of the basic timestamp ordering algorithm via Markov modeling," *Performance Evaluation 12* (1991), 17-41.

[SiSm94]   V. Singhal and A. J. Smith. "Characterization of contention in real relational databases," *Technical Report UCB/CSD 94/801*, Computer Science Division, University of California at Berkeley, March 1994.

[SiYL94]   M. Singhal, Y. Yesha, and M. T. Liu. "Probabilistic analysis of transaction blocking under arbitrary data access distribution in database systems," *Information Sciences 78*,3-4 (1994), 161-187.

[SkZd89]   A. H. Skarra and S. B. Zdonik. "Concurrency control and object-oriented databases," in *Object-Oriented Concepts, Databases, and Applications*, W. Kim and F. H. Lochovsky (Editors), ACM Press, 1989, pp. 395-421.

[SLSP95]   D. Shasha, F. Llirbat, E. Simon, and P. Valduriez. "Transaction chopping: Algorithms and performance studies," *ACM Transactions on Database Systems 20*,3 (September 1995), 325-363.

[SoSh90]   N. Soparkar and A. Silberschatz. "Data partitioning and virtual messages," *Proceedings 9th Symposium on Principles of Database Systems*, Nashville, TN, April 1990, pp. 344-356.

[SrCa93]   V. Srinivasan and M. J. Carey. "Performance of B+ tree concurrency control algorithms," *Very Large Data Base Journal 2* (1993), 361-406.

[Stew78]   W. J. Stewart. "A comparison of numerical techniques in Markov modeling," *Communications of the ACM 21*,2 (February 1978), 144-152.

[TaGS85]   Y. C. Tay, N. Goodman, and R. Suri. "Locking performance in centralized databases," *ACM Transactions on Database Systems 10*,4 (December 1985), 415-462.

[Tasa86]   S. Tasaka. *Performance Analysis of Multiple Access Protocols*, MIT Press, 1986.

[TaSG85]   Y. C. Tay, R. Suri, and N. Goodman. "A mean value performance model for locking in databases," *Journal of the ACM 32*,3 (July 1985), 618-651.

[TayY87]   Y. C. Tay. *Locking Performance in Centralized Databases*, Academic Press, 1987.

[TayY90]   Y. C. Tay. "Issues in modeling locking performance," in *Stochastic Analysis of Computer and Communication Systems*, H. Takagi (Editor), North-Holland, 1990, pp. 631-658.

[TCG+92]   A. Tansel, J. Clifford, S. Gadia, S. Jajodia, A. Segev, and R. Snodgrass (Editors). *Temporal Databases: Theory, Design, and Implementation*. Benjamin Cummings, 1993.

[ThBa84]   A. Thomasian and P. Bay. "Analysis of queueing network models with population size constraints and delayed blocked customers," *Proceedings 1984 ACM SIGMETRICS Conference on Measurement and Modeling of Computer Systems*, Boston, MA, August 1984, pp. 202-216.

[ThNa81]   A. Thomasian and B. Nadji. "Algorithms for queueing network models of multiprogrammed computers using generating functions," *Computer Performance 2*,3 (September 1981), 100-123.

[ThNa93]   A. Thomasian and B. Nadji. "State representation tradeoffs in Markov chain models for serialization delays in computer systems," *Computer Systems Science and Engineering 8*,3 (July 1993), 154-165.

[ThNi93]   A. Thomasian and V. Nicola. "Performance evaluation of a threshold method for scheduling readers and writers." *IEEE Transactions on Computers 42*,1 (January 1993), 83-98.

[Thom82]   A. Thomasian. "An iterative solution to the queueing network model of a DBMS with dynamic locking," *Proceedings 13th Computer Measurement Group Conference*, San Diego, CA, December 1982, pp. 252-261.

[Thom85]   A. Thomasian. "Performance evaluation of centralized databases with static locking," *IEEE Transactions on Software Engineering 11*,2 (April 1985), 346-355.

[Thom87]   A. Thomasian. "A performance study of dynamic load balancing in distributed systems," *Proceedings 7th International Conference on Distributed Computing Systems*, West Berlin, Germany, September 1987, IEEE Computer Society Press, pp. 178-185.

[Thom92a]   A. Thomasian. "Distributed optimistic concurrency control methods for high performance transaction processing," *IBM Research Report RC 17815*, Hawthorne, NY, March 1992 (submitted for publication).

[Thom92b]   A. Thomasian. "Performance analysis of locking policies with limited wait depth," *Proceedings Performance 92 and ACM*

SIGMETRICS Joint Conference Conference on Measurement and Modeling of Computer Systems, Newport, RI, June 1992, pp. 115-127.

[Thom93a] A. Thomasian. "On the number of remote sites accessed in distributed transaction processing," *IEEE Transactions on Parallel and Distributed Systems 4,*1 (January 1993), 99-103.

[Thom93b] A. Thomasian. "Two-phase locking and its thrashing behavior," *ACM Transactions on Database Systems 18,*4 (December 1993), 579-625.

[Thom94a] A. Thomasian. "On realistic modeling and analysis of lock contention," *Proceedings 10th International Conference on Data Engineering,* Houston, TX, February 1994, IEEE Computer Society Press, pp. 2-9.

[Thom94b] A. Thomasian. "A fractional data allocation method for distributed databases," *Proceedings 3rd International Conference on Parallel and Distributed Information Systems,* Austin, TX, September 1994, IEEE Computer Society, pp. 168-175.

[Thom95a] A. Thomasian. "Priority queueing in RAID5 disk arrays with an NVS cache," *MASCOTS'95: International Workshop on Modeling, Analysis and Simulation of Computer and Communication Systems,* Durham, NC, January 1995, pp. 168-172.

[Thom95b] A. Thomasian. "Performance analysis of locking policies with limited wait depth," *IBM Research Report RC 19977,* Hawthorne, NY, March 1995 (submitted to *Performance Evaluation).*

[Thom95c] A. Thomasian. "Realistic modeling of lock contention and its analysis," *Information Systems,* to appear, (also *IBM Research Report RC 19978,* Hawthorne, NY, March 1995).

[Thom95d] A. Thomasian. "Checkpointing for optimistic concurrency control methods." *IEEE Transactions on Knowledge and Data Engineering 7,*2 (April 1995), 332-339.

[Thom96] A. Thomasian. "A performance comparison of locking policies with limited wait depth," *IEEE Transactions on Knowledge and Data Engineering,* to appear (also *IBM Research Report RC 19967,* Hawthorne, NY, February 1993).

[ThRa90] A. Thomasian and E. Rahm. "A new distributed optimistic concurrency control method and a comparison of its performance with two-phase locking," *Proceedings 1990 International Conference Distributed Computing Systems,* Paris, France, May 1990, IEEE Computer Society Press, pp. 294-301.

[ThRy83] A. Thomasian and I. K. Ryu. "A decomposition solution to the queueing network model of the centralized DBMS with static locking," *Proc ACM SIGMETRICS Conference Conference on Measurement and Modeling of Computer Systems,* Minneapolis, MN, August 1983, pp. 82-92.

[ThRy86]   A. Thomasian and I. K. Ryu. "Performance comparison of concurrency control methods for shared centralized databases," Unpublished report, IBM T. J. Watson Research Center, Hawthorne, NY, 1986 (available from the first author).

[ThRy89]   A. Thomasian and I. K. Ryu. "A recursive solution method to analyze the performance of static locking systems," *IEEE Transactions on Software Engineering 15*,10 (October 1989), 1147-1156.

[ThRy91]   A. Thomasian and I. K. Ryu. "Performance analysis of two-phase locking," *IEEE Transactions on Software Engineering 17*,5 (May 1991), 386-402.

[Triv82]   K. S. Trivedi. *Probability and Statistics with Reliability, Queueing, and Computer Science Applications,* Prentice-Hall, 1982.

[TsPH86]   J. Tsitsiklis, C. H. Papadimitriou, and P. Humblet. "The performance of a precedence-based queueing discipline," *Journal of the ACM 33*,3 (July 1986), 593-602.

[WeHa93]   G. Weikum and C. Hasse. "Multilevel transaction management for complex objects: Implementation, performance, parallelism," *Very Large Data Base Journal 2* (1993), 407-453.

[Weil88]   W. E. Weihl. "Commutativity based concurrency control for abstract data types" *IEEE Transactions on Computers 37*,12 (December 1988), 1488-1505.

[Weik91]   G. Weikum. "Principles and realization strategies of multilevel transaction management," *ACM Transactions on Database Systems 16*,4 (March 1991), 132-180.

[WeZo86]   H. Wedekind and G. Zoerntlein. "Prefetching in real-time database applications," *Proceedings 1986 ACM SIGMOD International Conference on Management of Data,* Washington, D.C., May 1986, pp. 215-226.

[WHMZ94]   G. Weikum, C. Hasse, A. Moenkeberg, and P. Zabback. "The COMFORT automatic tuning project, *Information Systems 19*,5 (1994), 381-432.

[YCDT89]   P. S. Yu, D. Cornell, D. M. Dias, and A. Thomasian. "Performance comparison of the IO shipping and database call shipping schemes in multi-system partitioned database systems," *Performance Evaluation 10*, (1989), 15-33.

[YuDa93]   P. S. Yu and D. M. Dias. "Performance analysis of concurrency control using locking with deferred blocking," *IEEE Transactions on Software Engineering 18*,10 (October 1993), 982-996.

[YuDL93]   P. S. Yu, D. M. Dias, and S. S. Lavenberg. "On modeling database concurrency control," *Journal of the ACM 40*,4 (September 1993), 831-872.

Index